Supporting and Sustaining Differentiated Instruction

An Administrator's Guide

Karen Hume

Toronto

Library and Archives Canada Cataloguing in Publication

Hume, Karen
    Supporting and sustaining differentiated instruction : an administrator's guide / Karen Hume.

Includes bibliographical references and index.

ISBN 978-0-13-812760-2

1. Differentiated teaching staffs. 2. Individualized instruction. I. Title.

LB1029.D55H86 2007   372.1102   C2007-905300-9

Copyright © 2008 Pearson Education Canada, a division of Pearson Canada Inc., Toronto, Ontario. Pearson Professional Learning. All rights reserved. This publication is protected by copyright and permission should be obtained from the publisher prior to any prohibited reproduction, storage in a retrieval system, or transmission in any form or by any means, electronic, mechanical, photocopying, recording, or likewise. For information regarding permission, write to the Permissions Department.

ISBN-13: 978-0-13-812760-2
ISBN-10: 0-13-812760-3

Vice-President, Publishing and Marketing, School Division: Mark Cobham
Vice-President, Marketing and Professional Field Services: Anne-Marie Scullion
Publisher, Pearson Professional Learning: Debbie Davidson
Director, Pearson Professional Learning: Terry (Theresa) Nikkel
Research and Communications Manager: Chris Allen
Project Co-ordinator, Pearson Professional Learning: Joanne Close
Developmental Editor: Elizabeth Salomons
Senior Production Editor: Jennifer Handel
Copy Editor: Martin Tooke
Proofreader: Laura Neves
Production Coordinator: Zane Kaneps
Composition: David Cheung
Permissions and Photo Research: Christina Beamish
Art Director: Alex Li
Art Coordination: Carloyn E. Sebestyen
Cover and Interior Design: Alex Li
Illustrators: David Cheung, Kevin Cheng
Cover Image Credit: Photodisc/Getty Images

For permission to reproduce copyrighted material, the publisher gratefully acknowledges the copyright holders listed in the source lines throughout the text as well as on page 170, which are considered extensions of this copyright page.

4 5   11 10 09 08

Printed and bound in Canada.

Contents

Introduction ix
Keep It Simple ix
Practise Simplicity and Synergy x
Start Where They (and You) Are xi
In and Out of Scope xi
How to Use This Guide xii

CHAPTER 1
What Is Differentiated Instruction? 1
Why Focus on Differentiated Instruction? 2
The Framework 4
Assessment, Evaluation, and Differentiated Instruction 6
Misconceptions About Differentiated Instruction 8
Teaching Adults: What Is Differentiated Instruction? 9
Process: Classroom Walk-Throughs 17

CHAPTER 2
Start Where YOU Are: Instructional Leadership Beliefs and Knowledge 21
The Principal as Instructional Leader 21
Quiz: Your Instructional Leadership Quotient 25
Finding Time: Prioritizing the Responsibilities of the Principalship 29

CHAPTER 3
Start Where They Are: Characteristics of Adult Learners 33
Adult Learners 33
Changing Minds 35
Supporting Change 39
Process: Workshop Assessments 43

Contents (continued)

CHAPTER 4

Planning Professional Learning 47

Professional Learning 47
Working with Data 50
Process: Creating a Professional Learning Plan 54

CHAPTER 5

Creating an Effective Learning Community 59

The Characteristics of a Learning Community 59
Your Role 61
Teaching Adults: Classroom Management and Organizational Procedures That Support Differentiation 63
Teaching Adults: Teacher Presence 66
Process: Encouraging Reflection 69

CHAPTER 6

Knowing Your Learners 71

The Strengths Revolution 71
Process: Acknowledging Staff Strengths 75
Teaching Adults: Introduction to Individual Differences and Sense-Based Learning Styles 77
Teaching Adults: Multiple Intelligences 82
Teaching Adults: Student Interests 87

CHAPTER 7

Essential Understandings 89

Getting to Essential Understandings 89
Teaching Adults: Essential Curriculum Outcomes 92
Teaching Adults: Essential Understandings and Questions 97

CHAPTER 8

Assessment for Learning (Pre-Assessment) 101

Pre-Assessing Knowledge and Attitude 101

Process: Pre-Assessing Teacher Knowledge Using Self-Reports and Quick Writes 103
Teaching Adults: Using Pre-Assessments to Group for Learning 108

CHAPTER 9

Powerful Instructional Strategies 115

Instructional Strategies 115
Process: Classroom Observation 118
Teaching Adults: An Introduction to the Top Nine Strategies 121
Teaching Adults: Similarities and Differences 124

CHAPTER 10

Appropriate Challenge Through Formative Assessment 129

Challenging Your Staff 130
Process: Providing Effective Feedback 131
Teaching Adults: Vygotsky and the Zone of Proximal Development 134
Teaching Adults: Providing Feedback 140
Teaching Adults: Formative Assessment 145

CHAPTER 11

Evaluating Fairly in the Differentiated Classroom 149

What Matters? 149
Teaching Adults: Addressing Teacher Concerns 152

CHAPTER 12

Where Are You Now? 155

References 159
Glossary 163
Index 165
Credits 170

About the Author

Karen Hume is a teacher, administrator, system leader, author, and keynote speaker. Her interest is in providing focused, practical, and inspiring support to teachers and administrators. After years of attending professional learning sessions directed toward someone's general idea of what the audience might need, Karen is passionate about personalizing, and helping administrators to personalize, the professional learning opportunities of educators.

Acknowledgments

Fingerprints are the perfect symbol of differentiation. No two prints are exactly alike, even in identical twins. They are the most notable indicators of our uniqueness. And they are consistent; fingerprints remain the same throughout our lives, making them, in ancient times, as valid as signatures on legal documents.

Fingerprints are also a perfect symbol for acknowledgments because this is a place where authors want to thank those individuals who have offered the unique and consistent support that only they can provide.

Thank you to the wonderful team in the Pearson Professional Learning Division—Vice President, Anne-Marie Scullion; Publisher, Debbie Davidson; Project Co-ordinator, Joanne Close; and Research and Communications Manager, Chris Allen. They all demonstrated huge commitment from long before the first word was written, and they continue to do so to this day. Thanks to Alex Li at Pearson for the great cover and interior design, to Craig Featherstone for his help with the Success for Every Student model, and to Jen Handel and the production team for tolerating an author with a not-so-hidden desire to dabble in layout and production.

I don't know if teaching skills and leadership skills are inborn or learned, but I do know that they emerge and develop through the opportunities that are afforded to us. My sincere appreciation is therefore extended to senior staff and to my teaching and administrative colleagues at the Durham District School Board. There are too many people to mention by name, but I do hope they all know how very grateful I am for the outstanding professional learning opportunities, ongoing support, and friendship offered so willingly over the last 20 years.

I am so lucky to have people in my life who provide unwavering encouragement and support. Just as we leave our fingerprints behind on everything we touch, the following people have made a significant and positive difference to me in this year of many "firsts." Forever thanks go to my parents, Gerri Hume and Ross Hume, and to my friends, Kim Airdrie, Roberta Dick, Brad Ledgerwood, Demetra Saldaris, and Eileen Sheppard. It is a pleasure to be able

Acknowledgments (continued)

to acknowledge and thank you for your many kindnesses through the tough days and the exhilarating ones.

The careful reading of this text by reviewers from across the country is gratefully acknowledged. A second reading will show you the many places where your insightful comments have made this a better guide.

Review Team

Christopher Atkinson, Literacy Mentor and Middle Level Writing Specialist
School District 6, Rothesay, NB

Dr. Michael R. Muise, Principal
Algonquin and Lakeshore Catholic District School Board (Kingston)

Marta Mulhern
Instructional Co-ordinator, Literacy
Peel District School Board

Diane Gagley, Consultant, Special Needs
Calgary Catholic District School Board

Don Gordon, Staff Development Co-ordinator for Middle School Curriculum and Numeracy K to 12
School District 43, Coquitlam

Ted Doherty, Superintendent of Education
Avon Maitland District School Board

Kathyrn D'Angelo, District Administrator, Learning Services
Richmond School District

Karen Bauer, High School Literacy Mentor
School District 2, Moncton

Susan Campbell, Literacy Supervisor, K to 12
School District 16, Miramichi

Jessica Kowall, Reading Clinician
Child Guidance Clinic
Winnipeg School Division

Sandra Pace, Superintendent of Curriculum
Director of Instruction for New Westminster School Board, District #40

Introduction

Keep It Simple

Humorist Mark Twain and mathematician Blaise Pascal both claimed that if they had more time, they would have written shorter letters. I always thought that was a clever, if not particularly meaningful, quip. Then I set out to write this book—a short guide for the busy school administrator, a guide that would be immediately useful, focused, practical; a guide that would distill my own work on differentiated instruction and that of others so that you would have exactly the information you need, exactly the processes you need, to support your teachers as they worked at developing increasingly effective and responsive classrooms. Along the way, I discovered the truth in Twain and Pascal's observation—a short book is more difficult and more time consuming to write than a long one. There is a fine line between simplicity and superficiality, and it is more challenging than you might expect to make everything "as simple as possible . . . but not simpler." As an avid reader of professional literature, it was difficult to review 10 books on collaborative culture and give you the single paragraph of information that I thought would be particularly helpful to a specific situation, or to boil the topic of pre-assessment in a differentiated classroom down to a single lesson plan and a process you could use to pre-assess teacher understanding.

I persisted because school administrators are incredibly busy people who are constantly being asked to take on more, to be more. The school effectiveness research of the mid '80s urged us to be "instructional leaders" (Cotton, 2003). That emphasis seemed to diminish as we turned our attention to, among other things, leading for change, increasing our emotional intelligence, developing professional learning communities, and making data-driven decisions. But now, if your district is anything like mine, there is a resurgence in the call for administrators to assume a greater leadership role in supporting and sustaining high-quality instruction in our schools. This, I think, is due in part to the data that tell us we are still striving to ensure higher levels of achievement by all students, and in part to the research-based instructional strategies that purport to make that difference. In the case of strategies, it is assumed that all teachers need to know them and be able to implement them effectively in their classrooms.

> "Everything should be made as simple as possible . . . but not simpler."
> —*Albert Einstein*

"The meeting's at 10. I'll send you a copy of the agenda, the hidden agenda and your personal agenda."

> "Simplicity is the ultimate sophistication."
> —Leonardo da Vinci

I won't attempt to hide my agenda. I happen to agree that most of us need to spend more of our time directly involved in activities that are going to have a demonstrable and significant positive impact on student achievement. However, I don't believe that simply being told that something is important and then being exhorted to do it is particularly helpful. Nor is it helpful to attend every district-led workshop that your teachers attend. It is high time that two "s" words of educational leadership made their way to the school office. The first word, rarely mentioned in the literature, is "simplicity"; the second, incessantly referenced in time-management writings, is "synergy."

Practise Simplicity and Synergy

Simplicity speaks to the core, the critical attributes, the essential understandings of a topic; synergy to working both efficiently and effectively such that the impact of your combined actions is greater than the sum of their individual parts. Have you tried to work synergistically on a dozen different initiatives? Were you as spectacularly unsuccessful at it as I was? The reason, I think, is in the "dozen different initiatives." Synergy, I'm convinced, is impossible without simplicity, for it is only when you can see the critical attributes and the commonalities among disparate actions that you can be focused and intentional, and thus save time.

Differentiated instruction is the ultimate topic for synergistic work in schools because it is not a program or even an initiative. Both words imply short-term add-ons to an administrator's or teacher's already overflowing plate of responsibilities. Differentiated instruction is a *comprehensive framework or organizing structure* for how all teachers in all subjects, K–12, understand and enact the teaching and learning in classrooms—*all* of the teaching and learning, not just the instruction that they differentiate. Differentiation always starts with effective instruction for the entire class, *and then* varies that effective instruction so it is responsive to the diverse learning needs and preferences of individual learners. The framework reflects an unequivocal focus on what matters:

- effective teaching that results in high levels of achievement for every student, and
- multiple points of entry to effective teaching so teachers can start where they are and, at a pace that works for them, increase both their overall effectiveness and their ability to differentiate

By becoming conversant with the differentiated instruction framework, you address all aspects of instructional effectiveness.

Start Where They (and You) Are

The concept of "start where they are" is central to differentiated instruction and to this guide. Brain research confirms that if you don't start where the individual is, there is no hope of learning, since all learning is built on prior understandings, but if you do start where they are, learning is all but guaranteed. This is true for learners of all ages and stages; not just the students in our schools, but teachers as they learn about differentiated instruction, and you as you develop or further your ability to be an effective instructional leader.

This guide will assist you as an instructional leader in two levels of differentiation:

- supporting teachers as they begin or continue to implement differentiated instruction in their classrooms, and
- helping you to be an effective instructional leader for any topic by learning how to differentiate the way you work with your staff

> "Human beings differ with their gifts and their talents. To teach them, you have to start where they are."
> —*Yuezheng in 4th century B.C., Chinese Treatise, Xue J*

IN AND OUT OF SCOPE

Project management experts remind us that it is as important to identify what isn't going to be accomplished (what is out of scope) as what is. That would seem to be even more important in a resource that stresses simplicity rather than comprehensiveness. Here is what *Supporting and Sustaining Differentiated Instruction: An Administrator's Guide* offers:

- essential understandings of effective teaching and differentiated instruction encapsulated in a series of 40-minute lesson plans that will help to ensure that your monthly staff meetings, divisional meetings, or professional learning community meetings are meaningful professional learning sessions
- models of the use of differentiated instruction structures in each lesson plan; later, you can transfer the use of these structures to topics of your choice
- completed, yet modifiable, PowerPoint slide shows, blackline masters for workshops, and forms for instructional and data-gathering processes
- data-collection and analysis suggestions to accompany each lesson plan that will help you to identify actions to look for as signs of effective differentiating, model the importance of evidence-based decision-making for staff, and understand how to identify helpful next steps for teachers

Supporting and Sustaining Differentiated Instruction: An Administrator's Guide does not

- negate the importance of job-embedded, sustained professional learning. If your staff meetings are currently focused on school organization rather than effective instruction, this guide will help you change that pattern, but workshops on their own don't make a significant difference to teacher practice. See Chapter 4 and the "Sustain the Learning" segment of each lesson plan for more information on how to provide effective support beyond the workshop.

- deal extensively with any one component of the differentiated instruction framework. For example, there are two lesson plans for the framework component of "Classroom Learning Community." You can choose a plan based on your analysis of staff needs, but even if you used both plans, you wouldn't meet the needs of a teacher whose classroom is chaotic and disorganized. This guide will, however, help you to more accurately define the areas of difficulty for a struggling teacher so you can obtain for them the focused, expert assistance they require.

- replace the in-depth study of differentiated instruction that is available if you conduct professional book clubs. For that, you may wish to refer to my professional book for teachers, *Start Where They Are: Differentiating for Success with the Young Adolescent*, or the e-book *Start Where They Are*, with its digital footage of classroom activity and author talk. (Note that both of these resources will be mentioned where appropriate in this guide, but they are completely optional.)

How to Use This Guide

The summer before I turned 13, my family took a long-awaited and much anticipated trip to Scotland. We rented a van, piled in the Scottish relatives, and travelled the countryside. Regardless of our direction of travel and whether we were on a busy thoroughfare or wending our way along dirt paths up the side of the Trossachs, there would be a signpost pointing in the direction of Crianlarich. In this guide, as in my travels through Scotland, all roads will take you to the differentiated instruction version of Crianlarich. Using simple data collected throughout the guide, you will decide where you are and where your teachers are right now for each component, and whether that means that you will be zipping along the four-lane blacktop or taking a more leisurely and scenic jog through the heather.

Begin by making that decision for the first four chapters based on where *you* are right now, not your teachers. Your destination at the end of Chapter 4 is a professional learning plan. Here is the content of Chapters 1–4:

Chapter 1   Definition of differentiated instruction and presentation of the framework. This is the first lesson plan of the book and the one you will probably want to use near the beginning of the school year. Misconceptions of differentiated instruction, the realities that counteract the myths, what to look for in your first walk-through

Chapter 2   Why instructional leadership matters, self-assessment of your instructional leadership quotient, how you find the time to lead, and who else should/could be involved

Chapter 3   Characteristics of adult learners, the implications of these characteristics for your workshops, how to assess participants' reactions and perceptions of learning, and the Concerns-Based Adoption Model of individual change

Chapter 4   Characteristics of high-quality professional learning, why you should offer whole-staff workshops when other forms of professional learning are more effective, how to work with data, and how to create a year or multi-year plan for professional learning about differentiated instruction

Chapters 1 to 4 provide a solid grounding in the essential factors of effective instructional leadership. You will be able to apply these factors at any time to the topics of your choice. Use the graphic on the following page to decide where you need to start.

Each of Chapters 5–11 then focuses on a different component of the differentiated instruction framework and contains one or more lesson plans for that component. You can use only the chapters that are relevant to you, and in the order that works for you. If you prefer to work sequentially through the book, you can choose a single lesson plan from each chapter and provide an introduction to differentiated instruction in a year. Or, you can delve into a component, taking as much time as needed. Flexibility is a key principle of differentiated instruction and of your use of this guide.

CHAPTER 1

What Is Differentiated Instruction?

CHAPTER AT A GLANCE

Section	Focus	Action/Time
Why Focus on Differentiated Instruction? (p. 2)	Importance of a shared framework Why differentiated instruction?	Read
The Framework (p. 4)	The *Success for Every Student* model of effective differentiated instruction For you—the *Success for Every Teacher* model	Read
Assessment, Evaluation, and Differentiated Instruction (p. 6)	Explains why the *Success for Every Student* model uses "evidence base" rather than the more common assessment terms	Read
Misconceptions About Differentiated Instruction (p. 8)	A chart of eight common misconceptions about differentiated instruction and the truths that counteract them	Read
Teaching Adults (p. 9)	Introduce differentiated instruction as a framework or organizing structure for effective, responsive teaching and learning Share three components of the *Success for Every Student* model. (Optional—share all components.)	40-minute session plus 30 minutes of preparation
Process (p. 17)	Classroom walk-throughs	5–10 minutes per classroom including notes of acknowledgment

MODEL FOCUS

Learning Community
Knowledge of Students
Teacher Beliefs and Knowledge

Why Focus on Differentiated Instruction?

Differentiated instruction is effective instruction that is responsive to an individual's learning needs, interests, and preferences. It is an ideal choice for a common, school-wide framework because it

- is about effective teaching and best practices
- applies to all grades K–12, including combined grades
- applies to all subject areas
- applies to a teacher's work with students and an administrator's work with teachers, allowing you to both model best practices and be more effective with your staff
- is not a program and therefore does not require expensive specialized resources or significant restructuring of current practices
- is comprehensive and therefore includes many assessment and instructional practices that your staff may already be using

Many research traditions inform differentiated instruction.

Finally, because differentiated instruction is a framework based on effective instruction, you will find tremendous value in applying its precepts to various school initiatives. For example, if your school has a focus on character education, test it against the elements of your differentiated instruction framework to ensure that your character education work meets the criteria of effectiveness; in other words, use the framework to tweak the character education program so that it meets academic as well as social, emotional, and moral goals. (For a specific example of character education applied to the framework, see *Start Where They Are*, pages 10–11.)

Michael Fullan (2001, p. 109) promotes the need for "coherence-making" as a way to get beyond "too many disconnected, episodic, piecemeal, superficially adorned projects." The differentiated instruction framework, as represented by the *Success for Every Student* model (see page 4), meets this need by providing all teachers with a shared language and a set of guiding principles, making the development of school-wide instructional practices possible. This, in turn, makes it much easier for staff to work together for the benefit of all students.

"We can ask our people to work eight days a week, but we'll have to pay a royalty to The Beatles."

From the perspective of the individual teacher, the differentiated instruction framework helps his or her teaching life to make more sense and be more coherent. Teachers will not need to juggle competing priorities because they will see where each priority fits into the overall framework and will be in a better position to work synergistically.

Learn More About Coherence-Making

Michael Fullan is acknowledged as the educational author who has written extensively about the importance of coherence-making within a school and across a system.

Fullan, M. (2001). *Leading in a culture of change: Being effective in complex times.* San Francisco, California: Jossey-Bass.

Fullan, M., Hill, P., & Crevola, C. (2006). *Breakthrough.* California: Corwin Press.

The Framework

This model is appropriate both to teachers differentiating effective instruction for students and, with a couple of small changes of perspective, to you differentiating effective instruction for teachers.

The ovals in the outer diamond represent the conditions of effectiveness that are the preconditions for differentiation:

- a focus on the essential understandings of the content (what is taught)
- teacher awareness of their beliefs and knowledge and the impact these have on their actions
- the development of a supportive learning community (the context in which teaching and learning take place)
- appropriately challenging goals and conditions that will result in increased achievement

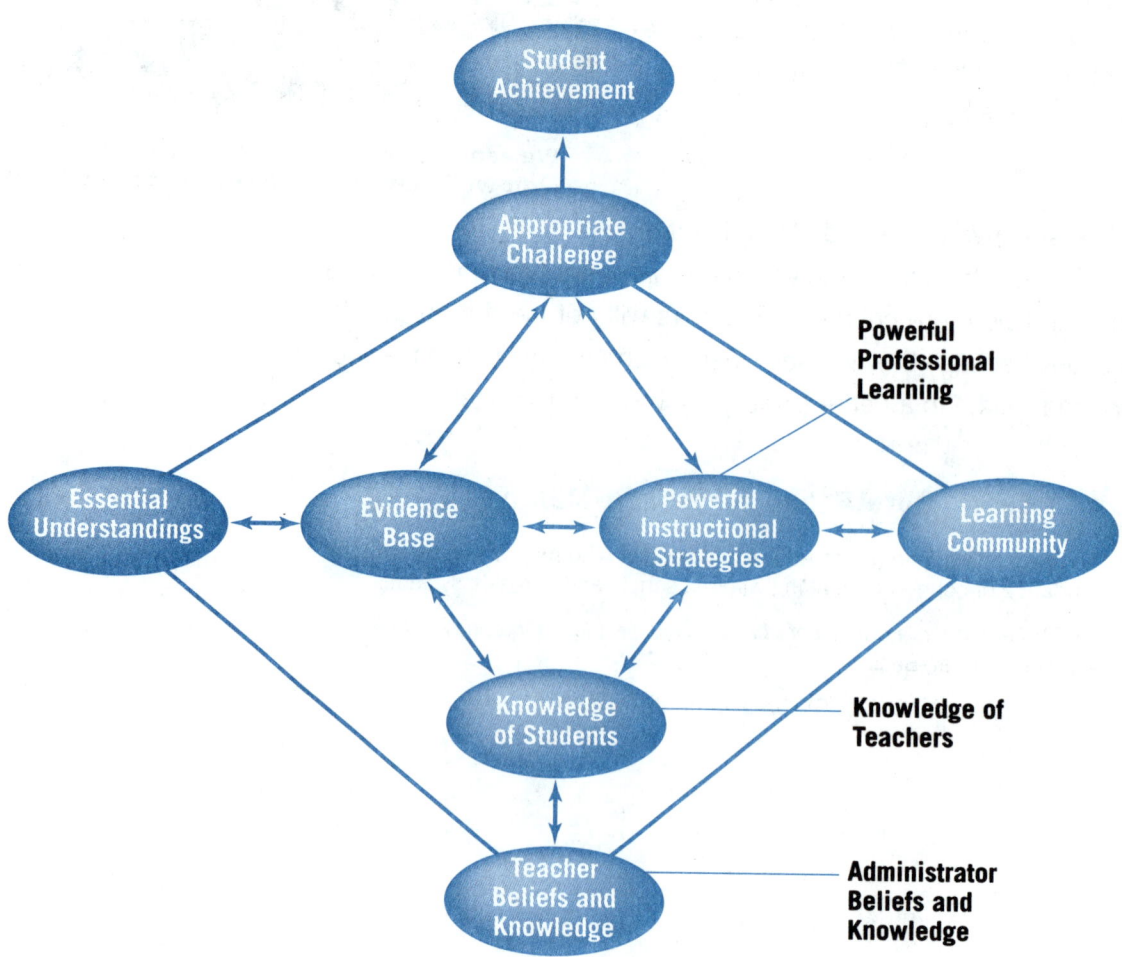

Success for Every Student (Success for Every Teacher)

4   Chapter 1

If these components are not in place, differentiation will not be successful. Differentiation is in *how* students or teachers learn, not in *what* they learn. The bottom line is this: You have to be an effective teacher before you can think about being an effective differentiated teacher. As you will see in chapters 2 through 7, this is as true at the school level as it is in the classroom.

The ovals in the inner diamond are the nuts and bolts of what is differentiated. The dynamic interplay of

- knowledge of the individual,
- powerful instructional strategies,
- a multiplicity of data sources in the evidence base, and
- appropriate challenge

highlights the fact that actions of differentiation are based on multiple points of reference. It is the multiple points of reference that initially make differentiated instruction a challenging concept for some teachers.

You may be familiar with Carol Ann Tomlinson's model of differentiated instruction (1999, p. 15). If so, Knowledge of Students (Teachers) encompasses the three aspects of the learner she says should be paid attention to when differentiating: interests, learning preferences (including learning styles, intelligences, gender, and culture), and readiness to learn a particular concept. The centre line is where her three categories of what can be differentiated in the classroom—content, process, and product—could be placed, recognizing that each of her categories requires all three of essential understanding, evidence base, and powerful instructional strategies.

To review the model, trace the inside diamond for the key components of differentiated instruction. To ensure you have the appropriate context to access the power of differentiated instruction, trace the outside diamond.

Finally, note the double-headed arrows: one between Essential Understandings and Evidence Base, and one between Learning Community and Powerful Instructional Strategies. Focusing on essential understandings determines what you gather in evidence of those understandings and how you gather that evidence. The evidence of understanding, in turn, determines what you do next to enhance that understanding.

Likewise, the strength of your learning community affects the powerful instructional strategies you will be able to use. At the same time, the instructional strategies you use influence the development of your community.

Assessment, Evaluation, and Differentiated Instruction

Several times each year, we review and sign student progress reports prior to sending them home to parents and guardians. In the course of that review, we usually learn more about the students in our school and we always learn more about the teachers. Student progress reports, while clearly not intended for this purpose, provide us with helpful evidence of teachers' beliefs, practices, and knowledge of assessment literacy. Simply by reading teacher comments on report cards, we get a picture of the kinds of activities that take place in the classroom, the forms of assessment teachers are using, and whether the teacher is using student strengths to enhance the learning of difficult concepts or is taking a more remedial approach.

Our understanding of our teachers' assessment practices is coming partially from the words or numbers in the reports we are reading, and partially from other sources, such as our observations in classrooms and casual conversation about assessment practices and beliefs as we relax with staff at the end of parent–teacher interview night. All of these sources constitute evidence or data that we use, consciously or not, to inform the next steps we take with each teacher.

Teachers, of course, do exactly the same thing in the classroom. They will use tests or performance-based assessments to gather information formally, but they also use the quizzical expression on the student's face to determine understanding, and the overheard comment to determine a misconception about a concept.

In the *Success for Every Student/Teacher* model, I have used the term "evidence base" to emphasize the fact that knowledge and awareness of the learner and of the essential understandings of the curriculum provides the teacher, whether classroom teacher or instructional leader, with myriad formal and informal ways to gather evidence or data. This information will tell us the learner's starting point for a particular concept or skill and make it easier to determine what we can do next with that individual. By considering all of the implications of the term "evidence" rather than "assessment," I think we reassure teachers that there are many simple and manageable ways to gather useful information, and we make the ongoing assessment of a student's understanding, knowledge, and skills a far less onerous task.

The term being used is, of course, far less important than the recognition that the three phases of assessment must drive instruction. Diagnostic or pre-assessment—a form of assessment *for* learning (see Chapter 8)—allows teachers, for example, to create the short-term flexible learning groups that are central to differentiated instruction or to structure an activity in response to student interest or background knowledge.

Formative assessment is ongoing and takes place alongside instruction. It is also referred to as assessment *for* learning because both formal and informal formative assessments provide teachers and students with specific feedback in order to guide teaching and improve learning. When "students personally monitor what they are learning and use the feedback from this monitoring to make adjustments, adaptations, and even major changes in what they understand" (Earl, 2003, p. 25), this is assessment *as* learning. As Lorna Earl suggests, this is our ultimate assessment goal because it results in a self-motivated and reflective learner. More information about formative assessment is provided in Chapter 10.

Finally, summative assessment, or assessment *of* learning, describes the assessment activities that are graded and shared so that all assessment users—students, parents, teachers, administrators, and superintendents—know the extent to which learning goals have been achieved. Summative assessment is discussed in Chapter 11.

If assessment is central to instruction in general and to differentiated instruction in particular, and if assessment should be planned at the beginning of a unit of study rather than tacked on at the end, why deal with assessment in chapters 8, 10, and 11? Why not begin this guide with such an important topic? There are two reasons:

1. Teachers need to experience the effective use of data to inform instruction, not just be told that it is important. The Build the Evidence Base segments of the Teaching Adults lesson plans allow you to provide this modelling through simple and straightforward data collection methods.

2. Differentiated instruction is based on knowing your learners. Some of that knowledge comes through standard assessment formats such as tests, but much of it comes informally through conversation and collaborative activity. If you stress assessement too soon, some teachers may default to what they know and, if that knowledge is of formal assessment structures, will miss the pleasure of getting to know the children they teach.

> "Leadership in the pursuit of assessment balance and quality begins with a guiding vision, clearly showing how assessment fits into effective instruction."
>
> —*Stephen Chappuis, Richard Stiggins, Judith Arter, & Jan Chappuis*

Misconceptions About Differentiated Instruction

The lesson plans in this guide will provide staff with the experiences and information that encourage a change in beliefs, if that proves to be necessary. In the meantime, and so that you are prepared for early questions, here is an at-a-glance list of some of the most common myths or misconceptions about differentiated instruction, and the realities that counteract them.

MYTHS AND TRUTHS ABOUT DIFFERENTIATED INSTRUCTION

Differentiated instruction...	Differentiated instruction...
✗ takes more time.	✔ takes a bit more time in planning until you get used to it, and the same or less time in implementation and marking.
✗ is the latest fad.	✔ is effective teaching that recognizes the learning needs and preferences of the individual. Hopefully that's not a fad!
✗ requires an IEP for every student.	✔ clusters students, when needed and appropriate, into three or four flexible short-term groups. It is not individual instruction.
✗ is for students who do not fit "the norm," i.e., special needs or ELL students.	✔ is for all students. Chronological age is the only "norm" that can truly be claimed in our classrooms.
✗ means that students in a classroom work on different outcomes or expectations, relative to their ability.	✔ does not include differentiation of expectations. All students work on the same outcomes.
✗ is a grading nightmare because students are doing different work.	✔ deals with common outcomes so the assessments can also be common.
✗ equals a chaotic, disorganized, unstructured classroom.	✔ requires that routines, procedures, and classroom agreements are in place.
✗ is old news. I have been doing it forever.	✔ means being effective and responsive in each component of the model. It is a philosophy of teaching and learning and therefore a lifelong journey.

TEACHING Adults

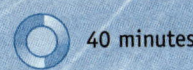
40 minutes

WHAT IS DIFFERENTIATED INSTRUCTION?

Significance to student achievement	If teachers are differentiating ineffective practice, you will see minimal growth in student achievement. This lesson highlights the difference between the achievement gain of a student with a highly ineffective teacher (14 percent) and a highly effective teacher (53 percent) (Marzano, 2003, p. 72), and makes the point that effectiveness is a precursor to differentiation. **effective:** having a definite or desired effect; powerful in effect; impressive—*Concise Oxford Dictionary*
Common questions and issues	• What is differentiated instruction? • Is "DI" the latest bandwagon? Am I expected to drop everything else I am doing to suddenly move in this new direction? (Any other misconceptions may also be voiced as a question.) • How does this initiative fit with our school's focus on _____? • Am I already doing this?
When would you use this lesson?	This session is foundational. It is one you will want to do with your entire staff near the start of a school year *if* you have decided that it is important for teachers to understand the framework. If teachers are going to misread the presentation of a framework as a sign they are moving into a huge new undertaking, you may want to modify this lesson, minimizing framework and differentiated instruction language and sharing only the positive actions you saw in the start to the new school year. If so, please read Chapter 4 to determine your next steps.
Materials you need	• photocopies of BLM 1.1 Classroom Walk-Through (1 per person) • photocopies of BLM 1.2 *Success for Every Student* Model (1 per person) • What Is Differentiated Instruction? PowerPoint presentation and equipment to show it. Note: If you decide to use the optional alternate ending (see page 15), please reorder the PowerPoint slides so that slide 1.12 comes at the end, after slides 1.13 and 1.14. • work kit (1 per table)

Materials you need (cont.)	• strips of paper for writing belief statements (1 per person) • material for posting belief statements, such as masking tape or push pins • lettering to spell out "[School Name] Teachers Believe . . ." (optional) • video segment showing the building of model from the *Start Where They Are* e-book, Chapter 1 (optional) • refreshments
Suggested group set-up	Teacher choice

Work Kit

Differentiated instruction requires a variety of resources. Model the organization and management of resources by developing work kits that you will use at each workshop. Invest in containers that store easily and allow you to see at a glance that all resources are in place. Ask a "materials manager" in each group to ensure that the work kit is complete before returning it to you. Items for the work kits include:

- pen (1 per person plus a couple of extras)
- set of fine point markers for mind mapping and detail work (1 set)
- set of chisel-point markers for flipchart work; try to get markers that do not bleed through paper (1 set)
- assortment of shapes and sizes of sticky notes, lined and unlined
- scissors (2–3 pairs)
- glue stick (1–2 large)

Build the Evidence Base

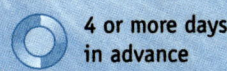
4 or more days in advance

1. Conduct a three- to five-minute walk-through of each classroom. See page 17 of this chapter for information on how to do a walk-through.

   The purpose of this particular walk-through is to
   - familiarize yourself with three of the seven components of the *Success for Every Student* model you will be sharing with staff
   - establish a baseline for your understanding of teacher beliefs and actions related to knowledge of students and development of a learning community
   - provide you with positive concrete examples of preconditions for differentiated instruction

2. Summarize the results of your walk-throughs for use in the lesson. The summary you share after this first walk-through should clearly communicate your desire to be a coach, not a judge. Prepare comments that will allow you to discuss the specific components of the *Success for Every Student* model. For example, when you are talking about knowledge of students, you might say something like the following:

   We all want to be "known," don't we? We all want to be seen as the individuals that we are, to be recognized for our strengths and our interests, to have people care about what we think and how we like to do our work. That's a truth of life, whether we are five or fifty-five. I was delighted to see all the different ways you are getting to know your students, everything from multiple intelligence quizzes (boy, we have a lot of kinesthetic learners!) to reading inventories, original poems about favourite memories, casual conversations, and asking students to vote for the genre of book to be read aloud. You will find that, as we work on differentiated instruction this year, your knowledge of students will become deeper and richer and, as you learn more about them, you will find it gets easier to plan lessons with the learning needs, preferences, and interests of your students clearly in mind.

   Notice that the sample does not include names. If you have a positive example from every class and can include all names without appearing insincere, by all means include names. Otherwise, it is safer to speak in general terms. This will especially be the case later in the year when you need to start including some requests for change along with your positive comments.

What Is Differentiated Instruction? **11**

Remember that walk-through summaries always protect negative comments from being attached to particular individuals. For example, never quantify by saying, "Two of our three primary teachers are looking forward to learning more about differentiated instruction," even if they have directly told you that.

Your walk-through summaries provide a critically important opportunity for you to build trust with teachers. Sosik and Dionne (1997, p. 459) define trust-building as "the process of establishing respect and instilling faith into followers based on leader integrity, honesty and openness." You build trust (Bridges, 2003, pp. 109–110) by

- honouring confidences
- doing what you say you will do
- listening to people carefully and telling them what you think they are saying
- looking out for your staff's best interests
- sharing yourself honestly; being transparent and "easy to read"
- asking for feedback on the subject of your own trustworthiness, and reflecting on the feedback that is given

Later, you will be inviting staff to assist you in summarizing teacher beliefs. At this point, just prepare your summaries of Learning Community and Knowledge of Students.

> *"He who mistrusts most should be trusted least."*
> —*Theognis of Megara*
> *Greek poet*

Learn More About Building Trust

William Bridges did much of the seminal work on management of the transitions between one situation and another. As he says (2003, p. 3), "It isn't the changes that do you in, it's the transitions....Change is situational....Transition, on the other hand, is psychological...."

Bridges, W. (2003). *Managing transitions: Making the most of change* (2nd ed.). Massachusetts: Perseus Publishing.

If you are interested in reading about one person's journey through difficult life transitions, William Bridges' autobiographical account is quite powerful.

Bridges, W. (2001). *The way of transition: Embracing life's most difficult moments.* Massachusetts: Perseus Publishing.

Teach the Session

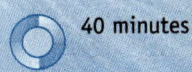 40 minutes

You could have the first slide displayed on the screen as a challenge for your teachers when they enter the room. You might want to require table groups to put forward one answer and give small prizes to any groups with the correct answer. However, before accepting answers from any group, show slide 2.

Accept answers from groups. The correct answer is: They are all ways of organizing information.

Ask for the benefits of organizing structures (saves time, provides focus, ensures that nothing important is left out, and so on).

Ask if anyone can identify the man (Francis Bacon) and explain why he's shown on the slide. (He attempted to reorganize all knowledge into a thorough and detailed system.)

Ask about any organizing structures teachers are aware of in education and if or how they are helpful to a teacher's work. (A couple of possibilities are Bloom's Taxonomy or Piaget's stages of development.)

Explain that the organizing structure you are going to introduce helps everyone to make sense of the school's various initiatives. On the second click, be specific about the initiatives in place in your school. Explain that the framework is about differentiating instruction to meet the needs of the individual learners in your school, but that, first, it is about effective education.

Explain that effective teachers have a significant impact on student achievement. Invite guesses as to the impact on a student who scores 50 percent on a test in September and retakes the same test in May. With the first click, present the statistic for an ineffective teacher (14 percent); with the second, the statistic for simply being a year older and having that additional year of life experience (6 percent); with the third, the impact of a highly effective teacher (53 percent).

Ask staff to think about the definition, focusing particularly on the word *effective*. Assure teachers that you know they work exceptionally hard and that you want them to be getting maximum impact from the work they do. Stress that overall effectiveness precedes everything, including differentiation.

At this point, you are ready to introduce the *Success for Every Student* model. If you have the *Start Where They Are* e-book, you can use the clip from Chapter 1 (page 7) to introduce the model for you. Stop the DVD at the appropriate spots to talk about each component as indicated in the PowerPoint notes below. If you do not have access to the DVD, you will be using PowerPoint slides 1.8–1.11 to explain the model.

Provide each staff member with a copy of BLM 1.2 and ask them to fill in the model components as you explain them.

Describe the *Success for Every Student* model as a double diamond. Explain that the components in the outside diamond are conditions for effectiveness in teaching. Note that the goal, always, is student achievement.

Talk about what you learned about the development of classroom learning communities from your walk-throughs.

Discuss the fact that differentiation does not mean individual instruction and that there are many activities that need to be done with the whole class. Stress the importance of community-building to students' sense of safety and willingness to take learning risks in the school.

Take a few minutes to have teachers share successful practices or humorous September stories, either as a whole group or in small groups.

Stress that learning-community work is foundational to effectiveness and to differentiation and, although it won't require the current level of intense work you know they are doing right now, it is important to maintain throughout the year.

Acknowledge that differentiation worries some people because they think it means 30 individual learning plans. Reassure your staff that it does not, but it does mean knowing students, and that you have seen good evidence of their work in this regard. Talk about some of the evidence you gathered on the walk-throughs that proves that teachers are getting to know their students.

Note that while teachers may not know all of the components of the model yet, they are central to each and every one of them. Go to the screen and demonstrate that you could draw a straight line between the teacher and student achievement, which shows that their beliefs and skills matter to every student in their care.

Ask staff to think about what you said about their development of a strong, positive learning community and their efforts to get to know each one of their students. Tell them you would like to start the year acknowledging the relationship between teachers' beliefs and the actions they take to benefit students. If there is time, give teachers a few minutes to write a belief statement that is reflective of their positive actions. Alternatively, if teachers need reflection time, ask that they complete this statement before the next meeting and begin the next meeting by having them share their statements with colleagues in small groups.

Note: If you choose the optional alternate ending to this session, use it now before showing PowerPoint slide 1.12 and making your concluding statements.

Thank teachers for an excellent start to the school year. Tell them that you will complete the model as you deal with the various components. Invite them to take the remaining components with them and decide themselves where each belongs. If you are using the clip from the *Start Where They Are* e-book, you can either pause after the first three components and finish the film next time, or show the entire clip (see optional alternate ending, below).

If planning for the year is going to take place soon, explain to teachers what will be asked of them. (See Chapter 4.)

If teachers are used to sitting with their friends or in certain spots in the room during staff meetings, you may wish to give them advance notice that an important part of differentiating instruction is the establishment of flexible short-term groups; that you will be making use of various groupings in future workshops; and that you appreciate their willingness to be flexible.

Optional Alternate Ending

Some of your staff may be "big picture" people and they will want to see the entire model in this first session. If you are using the clip from the *Start Where They Are* e-book, you can show the entire clip at this point. It will only take a couple of minutes.

If using the PowerPoint slides, invite teachers to review the component terms listed at the bottom of BLM 1.2 and to tell you which two components complete the outside diamond. On the first click, Essential Understandings will be filled in. Explain that essential understandings are important for all students and are not differentiated. Note that this statement means that assessment in a differentiated classroom is not as difficult as we might think, because the expectations or outcomes are consistent for all.

On the second click, Appropriate Challenge appears in the oval below Student Achievement. Explain that Appropriate Challenge is the one component that is part of both the outside and the inside diamonds. You might want to mention that Appropriate Challenge describes some of the art of teaching—being able to pitch instruction to the needs, interests, and learning preferences of the individual. Comment that Appropriate Challenge is also in the outer diamond because no one expects that the challenge be offered to one individual at a time. Explain that differentiated instruction makes extensive use of flexible, short-term learning groups so there are rarely more than two variations provided for any given activity.

The final slide for the model puts Evidence Base and Powerful Instructional Strategies in the inside ovals and inserts any missing double-headed arrows. Explain that Evidence Base refers to all forms of assessment, and that Powerful Instructional Strategies relates to some exciting research work done by Robert Marzano and colleagues. Reassure teachers that there will be plenty of time to work with all components.

Sustain the Learning

Read Chapter 4 and, using whatever process works for you, invite teacher involvement in determining the order and depth of work on various components of the differentiated instruction framework.

Reflect on the growth in your understanding of teachers as individuals and the growth in the development of your school's learning community because of the walk-throughs and your leadership in the session you just completed. Congratulations!

Include information gathered from your walk-throughs in your beginning-of-year family newsletter and distribute.

PROCESS: CLASSROOM WALK-THROUGHS

What Are They?

Walk-throughs are snapshots of the teaching and learning taking place in each and every classroom of your school.

> 3–5 minutes per classroom, once or twice a month

Why Do Them?

- Individual classroom snapshots provide you with a monthly photo album of the teaching and learning that is taking place in your school.
- Your presence in the classroom sends a message to students that learning is a priority.
- Your presence in the classroom sends a message to staff that teaching and learning are priorities. (Unlike students, they know how busy you are, so this is even more meaningful to them than to the students.)
- Walk-throughs maintain the school's focus on student achievement by keeping it front and centre in minds and actions.
- Talking with individuals or your whole staff after walk-throughs allows you to cross-pollinate ideas without putting any one teacher on the spot.
- You demonstrate authentic use of data by using results of the walk-throughs to modify professional learning sessions and to structure reflective conversations.
- Walk-throughs will help to inform your decision-making regarding school improvement practices.
- Teachers see you as more effective when you spend time in their classrooms and engage them in discussion about teaching and learning.

TIME MANAGEMENT TIP
Put walk-throughs in your schedule or they won't happen.

Steps in a Walk-Through

Review the walk-through observation form (BLM 1.1) and make a sufficient number of copies. The form is just for your use, *not* to give to teachers.

1. Walk into each classroom as unobtrusively as possible. During a walk-through, you should stay unobtrusive; complete the observation form after you leave the classroom.

2. In the walk-through, look for evidence of

   - student ownership of the learning environment:
     - posted student work
     - posters or artifacts that reflect student interests
     - student interpretations—written or verbal—of classroom agreements and routines

   - classroom organization that supports community development:
     - a comfortable seating area
     - signs of group work—group assignments, literature circle group lists, multiple bins of similar resources
     - seating arrangements that allow for a variety of student work groups, including individuals, partnerships, and small groups

   - the teacher getting to know students and helping them get to know each other
     - references—on the wall or in discussion with students—to uniqueness of learners, various learning styles, multiple intelligences, or student interests and background experiences
     - positive student responses, including examples, provided to your question about whether their teacher and classmates are getting to know them
     - students asking one another for assistance

3. Note the level of student engagement as you enter the room. On a scale of none to all, how many students seem engaged in the learning?

4. Literally, walk the entire room. A good way to remind yourself to do this is to mentally touch each of the four walls.

5. Stop beside a couple of students and quietly ask them the questions noted on your observation form.

6. Leave the classroom and complete your observation form in the hallway before moving on to the next class.

7. Send the teacher an email or put a thank-you note in their mailbox immediately after completing the walk-throughs or, if you are unavoidably delayed, by the end of the day. This is essential for good communication and an atmosphere of appreciation for teachers.

Note: If you would like to practise a walk-through, use a copy of the observation form (BLM 1.1) and the clip on the CD, "Walk-Through Practice," to do a virtual walk-through of Kelly's Grade 8 class.

When Do You Do Them?

Vary the day of the week and the time of day so you see a variety of subject areas and levels of student engagement.

Who Does Them?

- Walk-throughs are a powerful process so never allow anyone else to do this task for you. That said, your administrative partner will also do walk-throughs, as will some board superintendents. Many schools are now involving teachers in walk-throughs.

- Walk-throughs are usually done alone. Observations of the same classroom by multiple participants can be compiled into a single report afterwards. If teachers are involved in walk-throughs, however, they will need to walk with you so you can explain the process and direct them as to what they should be observing.

Q & A: WALK-THROUGHS

Q. What if teachers are resistant to my presence in their classroom?

A. Explain to staff in advance that you will be doing walk-throughs in order to get a school-wide view of teaching and learning, and that you are not there to conduct formal evaluations. Most staff will appreciate the interest you take in their work. However, if there is continued resistance, you need to work at developing their trust in you. Continue with walk-throughs, making sure your comments afterwards exclusively recognize positive actions. Staff should come to consider your walk-throughs as supportive rather than evaluative.

Q. Should I ignore any ineffective practices that I see?

A. Since your focus is on the photo album (whole school) rather than the individual snapshot (classroom), your sharing of reflections is initially whole-group and should be predominantly positive. Once teachers recognize that your role during walk-throughs is that of coach rather than evaluator, you will be able to move into reflective conversations (see page 70) with individuals where you can discuss individual concerns.

Q. Should I avoid walk-throughs with below-standard teachers?

A. When a teacher is below standard, your focus is on getting that teacher assistance to develop missing competencies and you make formal observations to document whether the interventions are working. If there is any possibility that the purpose of a walk-through and the purpose of a performance appraisal could be blurred, it might be best to avoid the walk-through. You are undoubtedly already spending more than enough time in that particular teacher's classroom to be able to fill in that missing snapshot.

Learn More About Walk-Throughs

Downey, C., et al. (2004). *The three-minute classroom walk-through: Changing school supervisory practice one teacher at a time.* California: Corwin Press.

CHAPTER 2

Start Where YOU Are: Instructional Leadership Beliefs and Knowledge

CHAPTER AT A GLANCE

Section	Focus	Action/Time
The Principal as Instructional Leader (p. 21)	The need for instructional leadership	Read
Quiz: Your Instructional Leadership Quotient (p. 25)	25 instructional leadership activities	10 minutes to take and score quiz
Finding Time: Prioritizing the Responsibilities of the Principalship (p. 29)	Finding the time to lead	Read

MODEL FOCUS

Administrator Beliefs and Knowledge

The Principal as Instructional Leader

The research is clear that teacher knowledge and skill level has a significant impact on student achievement (Darling-Hammond, 1997; Haycock, 1998; Cotton, 2003; Marzano, 2003). As teacher efficacy studies indicate, the better teachers get, the smarter their kids get. Unfortunately, the reverse can also be true. An ineffective teacher can impede a student's learning.

Teacher quality in any school varies, with most teachers falling somewhere near the middle on a continuum from highly ineffective to highly effective. While highly effective teachers require a very different kind of support and assistance from those who are less effective, every teacher, just like every student, needs both appropriate challenge and timely feedback if he or she is to have maximum positive impact on student achievement.

> "It is the principal's leadership, or lack of it, that determines whether teachers grow intellectually, a prerequisite to increasing student achievement."
>
> —*Hayes Mizell*

> "Example is not the main thing in influencing others. It is the only thing."
> —*Albert Einstein*

You are in an ideal position to support your teachers' learning and to encourage their professional growth. Your active involvement in the curricular and instructional life of your school is key to its effectiveness and to your own (Cotton, 2003); you have the positional authority to remove a number of barriers that teachers might face as they adopt new practices, and you gain even greater legitimacy in the eyes of your staff when you are supporting them in joining pedagogy with in-the-classroom practice.

Consider Thomas Sergiovanni's Leadership Forces Hierarchy (2007, p. 12). Sergiovanni does not like the term "instructional leadership," preferring in its place, "principal-teacher," which he thinks has a softer, kinder suggestion of "we're all in this together" rather than leader/follower. The argument can be made that "principal-teacher" is actually much tougher than "instructional leader" because it requires that principals be teachers who lead by example. Regardless of the term used, Sergiovanni maintains that what he is referring to as "educational leadership" is essential to a competent and effective school.

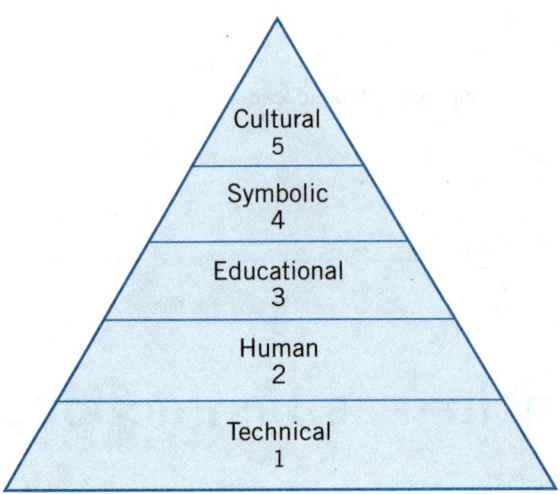

Leadership Forces Pyramid

Leadership Forces

Force	Examples	Reactions	Link to Excellence
1. Technical	• Plan, organize, coordinate, and schedule. • Manipulate strategies and situations to ensure optimum effectiveness.	People react to efficient management with indifference but have a low tolerance for inefficient management.	Presence is important to achieve and maintain routine school competence, but is not sufficient to achieve excellence. Absence results in school ineffectiveness and poor morale.

Leadership Forces (continued)

Force	Examples	Reactions	Link to Excellence
2. Human	• Provide needed support. • Encourage growth and creativity. • Build and maintain morale. • Use participatory decision-making.	People achieve high satisfaction of their interpersonal needs. They like the leader and the school, and respond with positive interpersonal behaviour. A pleasant atmosphere exists that facilitates the work of the school.	See 1. Technical.
3. Educational	• Diagnose educational problems. • Counsel teachers. • Provide supervision and evaluation. • Provide inservice. • Develop or implement provincial curriculum.	People respond positively to the strong expert power of the leader and are motivated to work. They appreciate the assistance and concern provided.	Presence is essential to routine competence and is strongly linked to, but still not sufficient for, excellence in schooling. Absence results in ineffectiveness.
4. Symbolic	• Tour the school. • Visit classrooms. • Know students. • Preside over ceremonies and rituals.	People learn what is of value to the leader and school, have a sense of order and direction, and enjoy sharing that sense with others. They respond with increased motivation and commitment.	Presence is essential to excellence in schooling though absence does not appear to negatively affect routine competence.
5. Cultural	• Articulate school purpose and mission. • Socialize new members. • Tell stories and maintain reinforcing myths. • Explain standard operating procedures. • Define uniqueness. • Develop and display a reinforcing symbol system. • Reward those who reflect the culture.	People become believers in a school as an ideological system. They are members of a strong culture that provides them with a sense of personal importance, individual significance, and work meaningfulness, which is highly motivating.	

Source: Adapted from Sergiovanni, Thomas. (2007). *Rethinking Leadership: A Collection of Articles*, 2nd ed. Thousand Oaks, California: Corwin Press, p. 16. Reprinted by permission of Corwin Press and Sage Publications.

The call for "instructional leadership," for want of a better term, frustrates and/or angers many school administrators. Some are willing to perform the role, but wonder where they could possibly find the time. Others argue that every action they take is, directly or indirectly, in the name of student achievement; that everyone in the school has a unique role to play and the instruction role belongs to teachers, whose instructional knowledge is current and who have credibility in the role.

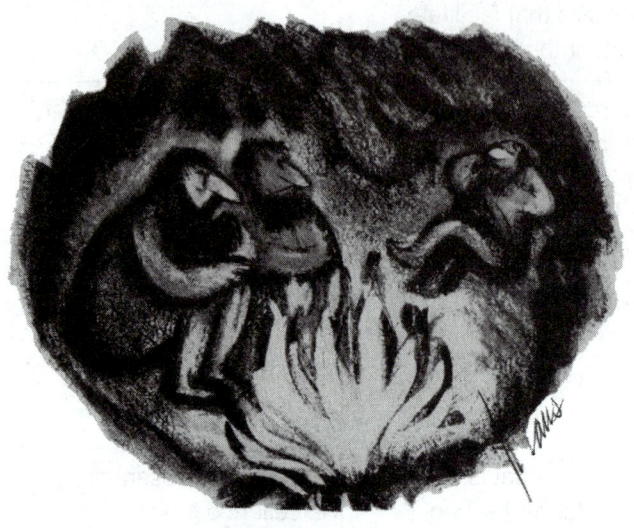

"Oh, I give him full credit for inventing fire, but what's he done since?"

© The New Yorker Collection, 1960, Robert Kraus from cartoonbank.com. All rights reserved.

Some of this last argument betrays a misconception about what instructional leadership looks like and who should be doing what. This is not surprising when the term is not well-defined and the most common examples are of teachers with encyclopedic knowledge and exemplary skills who have been released from their classrooms to serve as school-based coaches or district-level consultants. If this is the image that describes your vision of instructional leadership, it needs to be immediately replaced by a vision that is both realistic and achievable. Take the quiz to determine your current level of involvement as *one* of your school's instructional leaders, and to establish reasonable goals for your work this year. You will notice that some of the quiz items would be appropriate to Sergiovanni's definition of educational leadership and some to symbolic leadership, thereby supporting both effectiveness and excellence.

Learn More About the Importance of Instructional Leadership

Lindstrom, P.H., and Speck, M. (2004). *The principal as professional development leader.* Thousand Oaks, California: Corwin Press.

Quiz: Your Instructional Leadership Quotient

Mark the appropriate category for each action. For any checkmark you make in the final column, also list the name(s) of the individuals who have or will be taking responsibility for that action.

Action	I do this	I could and would do this if I had the time	Someone else does this or needs to do this
1. Ensure that teachers have the resources they need.			
2. Participate in professional learning sessions (beyond "dropping in").			
3. Establish coaching relationships among teachers.			
4. Engage in frequent classroom walk-throughs and observations.			
5. Give feedback to teachers as a result of your observations.			
6. Have conversations that are focused on instruction.			
7. Model the use of research-based instructional strategies at staff meetings.			
8. Teach teachers about instructional and/or assessment practices.			
9. Know and use the principles of adult learning when working with teachers.			
10. Know each teacher's current level of understanding regarding a specific instructional initiative, their learning preferences, and/or their teaching style.			
11. Arrange for teachers to participate in professional learning activities directly relevant to what they individually need to further their content knowledge and use of research-based instructional strategies.			

Start Where YOU Are

Action	I do this	I could and would do this if I had the time	Someone else does this or needs to do this
12. Stay informed about current research on effective schools.			
13. Provide teachers with research on instruction and effectiveness.			
14. Initiate contact with families around issues of student achievement.			
15. Monitor student progress, at both the classroom and the individual level, and report findings.			
16. Disaggregate data to determine the strengths and weaknesses of different sub-groups of students.			
17. Make decisions based on analysis and interpretation of school data and on research.			
18. Facilitate collaborative efforts among teachers.			
19. Be directly involved in helping teachers design curricular activities or address instructional issues.			
20. Recognize teachers' efforts to use new knowledge and strategies.			
21. Maintain your own and your teachers' attention on established instructional goals.			
22. Protect instructional time.			
23. Create experiences for teachers to serve as instructional leaders.			
24. Ensure that teachers address essential content.			
25. Establish a norm of continuous improvement.			

Source: Compiled from Marzano, Waters, & McNulty, 2005; Cotton, 2003; Blase & Blase, 1999; Glickman, Gordon, & Ross-Gordon, 1995; Smith & Andrews, 1989.

Scoring

Tally the number of checkmarks in each of the columns and multiply by four to calculate the percentage.

I do this	
I could and would do this if I had the time	
Someone else does this or needs to do this	

Review the results.

- Where are the majority of your checkmarks? Are you comfortable with your degree of involvement in instructional leadership actions?

- Are there any actions that need to be done by others, but currently are not? How will you address these?

- Which of the actions in the "I could and would do this if I had the time" column would you like to incorporate into your work this year?

In a survey of educational leaders, Doug Reeves (2004, p. 3; reported in Lovely, 2006, p. 24) found the following knowing–doing gaps:

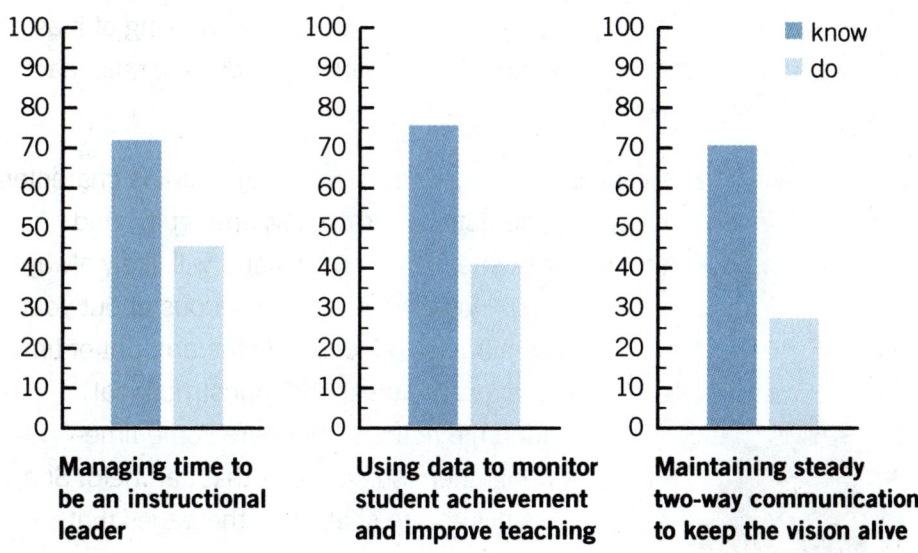

Source: Reeves, 2004 and Lovely, 2006.

The only place where this knowing–doing gap does not exist is in school operations and discipline—the place where administrators tend to spend most of their time and, not coincidentally, where failures to manage effectively bring about the most public criticism. Combine this reality with others: the fact that principal preparation programs claim to train for instructional

> "I was gratified to be able to answer promptly and I did. I said I didn't know."
> —*Mark Twain*

leadership but do not; that many administrators have been out of the classroom for a number of years; and that some of us, perhaps many of us, prefer administrative and managerial activities to instructional ones—and we have a dilemma of mammoth proportions.

I know of only three ways to address this dilemma:

1. Recognize that, just as you should not abdicate from all instructional leadership responsibilities, you should not own the role 100 percent. Teacher leaders, professional learning community members, divisional chairs, coaches, and school-based or district-level consultants all have a role to play, as indicated in the quiz you completed above, and in the plans you will make in Chapter 4.

2. Recognize that all you can do—all *anyone* can do—is start where they are and build from that point. If last year you were involved in 9 of the 25 instructional actions in the quiz, make it 11 this year, and a baker's dozen next year. Rely on study groups, peer coaches, monthly principals' meetings, district inservices, professional literature, and/or field trips to other schools to build your repertoire of strategies, to problem-solve for difficulties, and to receive the collegial support you need in order to keep supporting others. When you read and talk with your administrator colleagues about ideas, you will find it much easier to gain perspective on your school because you will be thinking of it as a system, rather than as a number of individual and idiosyncratic teachers and classrooms.

3. Carefully examine your use of time. "Principals' daily work is characterized by brevity, variety, fragmentation, complexity, ambiguity, and uncertainty" (Peterson and Cosner, 2005, p. 29) and will likely always be so. However, if you are serious about your commitment to increasing the amount of time and energy you expend in instructional leadership actions, there are some time-management suggestions that can help. Some possibilities are shared on the pages that follow.

"Time management is a myth! If I had any control over time, I'd still be sixteen and weigh 90 pounds!"

Finding Time: Prioritizing the Responsibilities of the Principalship

The Pareto Principle, also known as the 80/20 rule, was developed by economist and sociologist Vilfredo Pareto who discovered that 80 percent of wealth is held by 20 percent of the population. The principle has been found to hold true in a number of other situations:

- 80 percent of car accidents are caused by 20 percent of motorists
- 80 percent of screening mistakes at the airport come from 20 percent of the baggage screeners
- 80 percent of your beer is consumed by 20 percent of the beer drinkers at your party

School leaders know that the 80/20 rule is also alive and well in education:

- 80 percent of discipline issues come from 20 percent of the students
- 80 percent of parent phone calls come from 20 percent of the parents
- 80 percent of co-curriculars are run by 20 percent of the staff

The Pareto Principle is often worded in its negative, and most humorous, form. It can be a great motivator, however, if you turn it on its head and ask, "What 20 percent of my actions will make a significant difference to the learning and professional growth of 80 percent of my staff, and therefore a significant difference to student achievement?"

When it comes to instruction, this question is more reasonable than it once was. It used to be that we did the best we could, but didn't know for sure what would work and what wouldn't. Now, however, we have all of the effective-schools work, such as Robert Marzano's analyses of 35 years of research, providing us with "remarkably clear guidance as to the steps schools can take to be highly effective in enhancing student achievement" (Marzano, 2003, p. 11). Effective teaching is now science, as well as art; we have useful, helpful information to share with teachers.

> "For the 80 percent of activities that give you only 20 percent of results, the ideal is to eliminate them. You may need to do this before allocating more time to the high-value activities . . . ."
> —*Richard Koch*

> "A few things are always much more important than most things."
> —*Richard Koch*

> "Effective principals do not allow managerial tasks to consume their days. They create adequate time to focus on being the instructional leaders of their schools. It is the key part of their job."
>
> —Paul Young

Make Instructional Leadership a Priority

Nothing will happen until you make instructional leadership a priority. Stephen Covey (Covey, Merrill, and Merrill, 1994) tells the story of a college instructor who filled a glass jar with large rocks, then asked his class if the jar was full. When his students stated that the jar was indeed full, he responded by adding handfuls of gravel until the jar could hold no more. He again asked if the jar was full, and this time his students hesitated. The instructor did the same with sand, and then water, each time asking his students if they thought the jar was full.

He concluded by asking his students what they thought his demonstration said about time management. One student suggested that no matter how full your agenda is, there is always time to squeeze in more. The instructor dismissed this idea. Instead, he said, the trick is to remember to start with the priorities—the large rocks. If you start with the smaller, less important tasks, you won't be able to fit in the larger tasks.

If you have not been getting to your instructional leadership actions, it may be because you have assigned higher priority to other activities or tasks, or have allowed other people to set your priorities. Sure, there are times when those priorities are beyond your control: when you are required to be at district meetings, for example, or when there is a crisis at your school and everything else has to fall by the wayside while you deal with it. But these are short-term issues; if they are not, if other people's priorities are defining your work agenda, ask yourself what contribution you want to make to education and take back control of your time. Stephen Covey calls it the "tyranny of the urgent" and Oprah and the self-help industry exhort, "You'll only be able to say no to time-wasters when there's a burning yes inside for what truly matters."

Label the rocks in your jar. If the instructional leadership actions you have committed to taking don't constitute one of your large rocks, assess the priorities you *have* labelled in terms of their impact on student achievement. Are they really a higher priority than instruction? Which of them can be delegated, diminished, or discarded?

If you are not sure, take the time to explore each priority. For example, one of your rocks may be student discipline. Track the amount of time you spend on discipline in a typical week, including the nature of each incident and the source of the problem. At the end of the week, analyze and interpret your data. If you find that most of your discipline problems are, say, with third-graders on the playground at morning recess, you can delegate the resolution of that issue to the third-grade teacher, whereas if you find that 40 percent of Mr. Smith's fifth-graders are taking turns being sent out of class every morning at 11:00 a.m. because they don't understand the math he is teaching, you may need to get involved.

Plan for Instructional Leadership

Schedule the instructional leadership actions you want to accomplish in a given day or week, rather than leaving them to be dealt with when you have spare time. As well, plan your instructional leadership actions for the time of day when you are at your best. If you know it is going to be a challenging day, plan to do them first.

At the same time, *don't* schedule every moment of your time. If only 50 percent of your day is scheduled, you will have time to deal with interruptions and suddenly pressing issues, perhaps even the occasional additional instructional action!

Organize Around Your Priorities

Organize yourself the night before. Leave your walk-through forms (see page 17), reflective conversation prompts (see page 70), or the latest research report on the centre of your desk and tuck the other items of your to-do list out of sight. You will have the forward momentum you need when you walk into your office the next day.

Set up a filing system—electronic or paper—and assemble the work kits described in Chapter 1 (see page 10). In other words, plan ahead—do whatever works for you to feel prepared, organized, and focused on instructional leadership.

> "We must learn to distinguish between what is merely important' and what is wildly important.'"
> —Stephen Covey

Identify and Deal with Drains on Time

Routine Tasks

Set aside two daily half-hour or hour periods to read and respond to email or to return phone calls. You are in charge of your time—not your computer, PDA, or voice-mail system. When dealing with mail, try to use the touch-it-once technique: act on, file, or toss every item as you read it.

Unexpected Visitors

Establish regular periods of time when you do not want to be disturbed, or when you do. Stand while talking, turn your desk away from the open door, or close your door and have your assistant advise people that you are unavailable. You can have an open-door policy much of the time, but if you have no control over your schedule, you will not have time for instructional leadership.

Nonstop Activity

When you are immersed in the adrenaline rush of nonstop activity, stopping for a few minutes and doing nothing may seem counter-intuitive, but it is a smart way to handle overload.

Start and End Meetings on Time

Do not allow other people's tardiness to alter your day. The people who arrive at the meeting on time will appreciate your sensitivity to their schedules, and all participants will hopefully return the favour by respecting your time.

Understand That Being Visible Will Save You Time

Being visible in classrooms is part of instructional leadership. It will also save you time because you will become aware of and, by your very presence, be able to prevent, if necessary, situations that might have taken more of your time later on. An added bonus is that time spent in classrooms reminds you of why you became an educator in the first place.

CHAPTER 3

Start Where They Are: Characteristics of Adult Learners

CHAPTER AT A GLANCE

Section	Focus	Action/Time
Adult Learners (p. 33)	Identifying their characteristics, with implications for your work as instructional leader	Read
Changing Minds (p. 35)	Two methods of changing your own or someone else's mind	Read
Supporting Change (p. 39)	Concerns-Based Adoption Model (CBAM)	Read
Process (p. 43)	Assessing participants' perceptions of learning during workshops	3–5 minutes per Teaching Adults session

MODEL FOCUS

Knowledge of Teachers

Adult Learners

Undoubtedly, there are teachers in your school who possess knowledge about classroom practice far superior to your own. You may recognize some of them as better teachers in only their first or second year of teaching than you were in your ninth or tenth year. That's fine. Remember, however, that most classroom teachers do not have superior knowledge or ability when it comes to teaching adults; that is an area of strength that, with a little effort, you can claim as your own.

Many people have had the experience of attending a workshop where they were expected to participate in the learning as if they were six, twelve, or sixteen years of age. While the intent—having you understand life from a student's perspective—may be laudatory, the experience is often irritating. Although they are participating in the session to learn, workshop participants are not oversized children. To an even greater extent than children, adults come to any learning experience with a strong need for relevant, immediately useful applications, which take into account their extensive experiential and knowledge bases and their individual learning preferences.

It is helpful to consider the four areas where all adult learners in your school—whether they be teachers, administrative assistants, custodians, bus drivers, parents, or you—need to connect.

> "The best staff development is in the workplace, not in a workshop."
> —Richard DuFour

> "Any group too busy to reflect about its work is too busy to improve."
> —Robert Garmston and Bruce Wellman

> "Teaching is the second most private act in which adults engage."
> —Richard DuFour

You are in an ideal position to help teachers make these connections through the day-to-day work of your school and through more formalized experiences such as the Teaching Adults lesson plans provided in this guide. As Michael Fullan (2001, p. 126) suggests, "Learning in the setting where you work, or learning in context, is the learning with the greatest payoff because it is more specific (customized to the situation) and because it is social (involves the group). Learning in context is developing leadership and improving the organization as you go. Such learning changes the individual and the context simultaneously."

Adult learners need to connect to…	You help make these connections on a daily basis by…	And when you are teaching by…
…their own experiences and knowledge	• knowing their areas of expertise and honouring that in your conversations or in asking them to assist others • distributing resources according to how the resource connects to a teacher's knowledge base, rather than generically to all	• building in partner, small-group, and large-group opportunities to share experiences and knowledge • providing for individual reflection time (This is especially important if people need to consider and possibly reassess their mental models. See page 37.)

Adult learners need to connect to...	You help make these connections on a daily basis by...	And when you are teaching by...
...other people	<ul><li>scheduling common planning times for like-grade partners</li><li>supporting interdisciplinary or cross-grade units of study and the subsequent need for collaboration</li><li>developing professional learning communities</li></ul>	<ul><li>providing partner and small-group activities, especially those in which the result is a group product or group response with input from all members</li></ul>
...their specific work	<ul><li>making ongoing use of data to link actions to results</li><li>supporting attendance at conferences and workshops directly tied to the specifics of each teacher's work (e.g., Grade 5 science)</li></ul>	<ul><li>ensuring that the content emerges from school and classroom data</li><li>providing a rich variety of real-life examples that allow teachers to see possibilities for their classrooms</li><li>involving teachers in the planning and delivery of workshops (See Chapter 4.)</li></ul>
...who they are as learners	<ul><li>understanding and responding to the learning preferences of individuals (See Chapter 5.)</li></ul>	<ul><li>instructing, and having participants demonstrate their understanding, through multiple modalities and intelligences (See Chapter 5.)</li></ul>

By paying attention to the four connections while engaged in any instructional leadership actions, you increase the likelihood that adult learners will consider you helpful and skilled in supporting their growth. This does not mean, however, that your path to an increasingly effective school will be problem-free.

Changing Minds

Instructional leadership actions must be focused on the improvement of student achievement. Rather than making workshop decisions based solely on what teachers say they would like or even what they feel they need, you need to work with your planning team to choose actions that address needs evident in your student achievement data. This sounds obvious and straightforward until you consider the fact that this means you are in the position of driving a professional learning agenda unlikely to be universally endorsed by everyone. As soon as you define a student achievement goal, all manner of objections may surface. You have likely heard variations of many of the following:

- That isn't the right goal. Achievement can't happen until our students feel better about themselves/develop learning skills/ . . . .
- It is the right goal, but some of our students will never achieve it. Home environment makes all the difference.
- Your data is incorrect. Not everything that counts can be counted.
- I am what I am (the Popeye defence); I teach the way I teach. I have standards to uphold and students will need to measure up.
- There is no time because of curriculum content/other initiatives/ . . . .
- This is what we have always done, packaged under a different name. The more things change, the more they stay the same.

None of these objections will be new to you, even if you happen to be new to administration. Each reflects a belief formed by an individual's history, experiences, and personality. Senge et al. (1994, p. 235) refer to these beliefs as our mental models: "the images, assumptions, and stories which we carry in our minds of ourselves, other people, institutions, and every aspect of the world. Like a pane of glass framing and subtly distorting our vision, mental models determine what we see." Mental models are exceptionally difficult to change. When presented with new information or a new way of doing something, we all tend to do our best to maintain our cognitive equilibrium by trying to make new information work with what we already know. If it is an easy fit, we accept the new information; sometimes we even allow it to expand and enrich our model. But if the information does not fit with what we believe, we have no choice but to either reject the new information or reject the way we view the world. I'm sure you can guess which one we choose!

If you have individuals in your school with dysfunctional or limited mental models of teaching and learning, they may be resistant to every positive suggestion for change. A few resisters, or even one resister with influence, can seriously damage morale and make it difficult for others to learn. You cannot afford to "just ignore" a resister. That said, we also need to recognize that resisters perform a useful function in our schools. They keep us honest and grounded in reality by reminding us of the very real difficulties of changing practice, and they make us better leaders because one of the best ways to deal with resisters is to be more open and transparent in our communications with everyone.

> "Faced with having to change our views or prove that there is no need to do so, most of us immediately get busy on the proof."
> —John Kenneth Galbraith

> "Like a photographer exploring various perspectives of a subject, each comment offers a picture from a different vantage point in an effort to tell the whole story."
> —Sherrin Bennett & Juanita Brown

Copyright Grantland Enterprises; www.grantland.net.

Some methods of dealing with resisters include:

- Determine the reason for the resistance and respond to it using the suggestions from the Concerns-Based Adoption Model (see this chapter, page 39).

- Alter the environment so that you are using the positive power of the group. For example, end Teaching Adults sessions with Round-Robin discussions in which each teacher gives one helpful idea they learned during the session. Even changing the seating arrangements so that participants are sitting in a circle can have a huge impact on group dynamics.

- Recognize the strengths of the resistant individual (see pages 75–76), and involve them in the change in a way that will make use of those strengths.

- Refuse to listen to claims that one individual is speaking for several people. Insist that each person speak only for themselves.

- Stay focused on your student achievement goal, recognizing the resister's objections as helpful in making invisible problems visible so that you can address them. If you look at the situation this way, you will find it easier to separate ideas from the personalities of the individuals who deliver them.

The goal, with resisters and with those at the opposite end of the spectrum who embrace change, is the same. We want people to be aware of their own mental models so they can decide if and when they need to alter those models. There are two ways that an individual can alter their mental model once they decide they are willing to do so. One is to engage in what Howard Gardner (2006) calls "mental surgery." This method involves knowing your own mind—what you believe and how you think—well enough that you can actively seek

Start Where They Are **37**

new information in a form that will be convincing to you. For example, let's say I am a teacher who favours whole-class instruction over differentiated small-group instruction, but my school has decided to support the latter. If I know that I am best influenced by research studies, stories of success from a colleague's classroom, or the opportunity to observe a colleague's class in action, I can take the appropriate action and significantly increase the likelihood that I will change my practice.

Mental surgery requires self-reflection (see page 70). You can encourage that behaviour in your workshops, but you cannot mandate it! What you *can* do, however, is provide new information in many different modalities to increase the likelihood that you will be sharing information in a form that works for the individual. That's one of the reasons that workshops need to be accompanied by follow-up work to sustain and embed the learning—there are only so many approaches that can be taken in a 40-minute session.

The other method of mind-changing is to act your way into new behaviours and a new way of thinking. That is really what this guide is supporting you in doing, especially if you are uncomfortable with teaching teachers. I am essentially saying, "Here is the information you need about differentiated instruction. It is accurate and it will be helpful to your teachers. Here is how you can personalize this work to the needs of your school, and here are a number of ways you can share and sustain it. Give it a try."

Acting your way in works for hands-on learners and for people working in an environment where risk-taking is encouraged and supported. If you truly want to remove the anxiety around potential failure that your staff may feel when learning something new, there is no better way than to model risk-taking behaviours yourself by taking instructional actions that are new to you, considering these actions an "experiment" and enlisting others—your administrative partner, planning team, or the entire staff—in providing you with feedback and support as you practise the new action. Then make the same process available to teachers by ensuring that you sustain their learning through engagement in various forms of learning communities. (See Chapter 6.)

> "To create real change in this world, you have to have a vision, and you have to have enormous perseverance. It's the same principle that applies in any entrepreneurial adventure: You've got to be too stupid to quit."
> —Marguerite Sallee

Learn More About Changing Minds

Gardner, H. (2006). *Changing minds: The art and science of changing our own and other people's minds*. Boston, Massachusetts: Harvard Business School Press.

Howard Gardner discusses the seven factors that change minds, including new resources that—confirming our experiences in schools—he says work on mind-changing only for a short time.

Supporting Change

Regardless of how commonsensical and reasonable your focus on the effective differentiated classroom is, how charismatic, inclusive, and supportive you are as an individual, or how useful and personalized your workshops, some teachers will perceive what they are doing as learning and professional growth, while others will still see it as an unwelcome challenge to their mental model. As instructional leader, you want to move all teachers forward in each component of the effective differentiated instruction framework. To do so, you are going to need to identify where each teacher is in terms of his or her stage of concern about each component and begin from that starting point.

This is not as complicated as it sounds. The Concerns-Based Adoption Model is a theory of change that provides not only an explanation of the stages of concern all individuals progress through when implementing a new innovation, but also a list of the instructional leadership actions you can take to provide support at each stage.

Concerns-Based Adoption Model: Stages of Concern About an Innovation

Stage	Label	Key Concern	How You Can Help
0	Awareness	What is it?	• Share enough information to create interest, but not so much that teachers are overwhelmed
1	Informational	What are the details? I need to know more.	• Provide accurate information in a variety of modalities. (See the Teaching Adults sessions in this guide.) • Be enthusiastic. • Help teachers identify the similarities and differences between new ideas and current practice.
2	Personal	How will it affect me?	• Build a comprehensive framework, one component at a time, to prevent information overload. • Use conversations and written notes to encourage teachers. (See pages 69 and 75.)
3	Management	Where will I find time to do this?	• Work on one component at a time and at a pace that is comfortable for all teachers. • After introducing each component, help teachers find solutions to deal with any time- or classroom-management concerns.

Start Where They Are

Concerns-Based Adoption Model: Stages of Concern About an Innovation (continued)			
Stage	Label	Key Concern	How You Can Help
4	Consequence	How would it affect my students?	• Share student achievement data during the Teaching Adults sessions and in family newsletters. • Provide teachers with positive feedback individually and during Teaching Adults sessions.
5	Collaboration	What are my colleagues doing?	• Provide opportunities for teachers interested in collaborating to work together. • Assist teachers with establishing norms and procedures that will support collaboration.
6	Refocusing	Why don't we consider doing . . . ?	• Provide resources and time for teachers who want to further improve the framework. • Help teachers channel their ideas and energies productively.

Adapted with permission from SEDL. Source: Hord, S. M., Rutherford, W. L., Huling, L., & Hall, G. E. (2006). *Taking Charge of Change* (Revised ed.), Austin, Texas: SEDL.

Copyright Grantland Enterprises; www.grantland.net.

 Although progression through the stages will not be lockstep, you can use multiple copies of BLM 3.1 to track the stages of concern your teachers are at regarding each component of the differentiated instruction framework and to plan actions to support individuals.

Determining an individual's stage of concern is as simple and straightforward as asking a few questions. For example, if you want to differentiate a workshop about diagnostic assessment (see Chapter 8), you can provide teachers with a survey form (BLM 8.1) with questions as basic as "Do you use diagnostic or pre-assessments before planning a unit?" and "What concerns you about pre-assessing students?" If the answer to the first question is "No," the teacher is at the awareness level. The answer to the second question may require a bit of interpretation but, given your knowledge of the individual and his or her teaching, should still be relatively easy to determine. For example, a response of "I am concerned that pre-assessments are useless because I am required to teach every outcome" may indicate a need for information or personal reassurance if it is coming from a new teacher, or it might be a justification of no action or indicative of a management concern if it comes from a teacher who finds responsive planning overwhelming.

The general survey questions, asked in writing or verbally, work well when you are gathering information prior to presenting a workshop, and can be used again after a period of implementation as a measure of growth. During implementation, or if you aren't sure what to make of a teacher's response, ask a few specific questions. Hord refers to these specific questions, casually and informally asked in the hallway or staffroom, as a "one-legged interview." Here is an example:

> *At your last workshop, you talked with teachers about determining student strengths and learning preferences, and making use of that information to differentiate instruction during one lesson each week for the next month. Halfway through the month, you come across fifth-grade teacher Jen Scottsdale in the workroom. "So how's the learning preferences work going with your class, Jen?" you ask. Jen's response is positive, if a little hesitant. "It's going well, I think," she says. "My kids certainly enjoyed doing the inventories."*
>
> *Noting the slight hesitancy in Jen's response and still unsure of where she is on the Concerns-Based Adoption Model, you ask directly, "What's concerning you about this work, Jen?"*
>
> *"It all just feels like a party game to me," Jen says. "I just don't see the point of my kids finding out that they like to learn kinesthetically. All that does is put pressure on me to teach that way, and I don't know any way to do that except in physical education class."*

From Jen's comment, you know that she needs personal reassurance and more information. Without understanding her concerns any more precisely than that, you are in a position to provide Jen with the support that she needs—*without* rolling up your sleeves and immersing yourself in Jen's classroom. Being an instructional leader is about supporting and sustaining your teachers in their work; you can't do that if you try to function as an instructional coach in every classroom. Instead, in response to Jen's concerns, you might arrange for her to talk with or observe a colleague who makes effective use of kinesthetic strategies when teaching spelling. (And you know which colleague to recommend to her from a classroom walk-through or from the one-legged interview you did what that teacher.) You might want to share the CBAM stages with her so she can look forward to moving from personal concerns (stages 0–2) to task concerns (stage 3)—because, once there, it is easier to move to the impact stages (stages 4–6) where Jen will experience the positive results of her work in terms of increased student achievement and will "own" the change she has made to her practice.

If you have worked through Chapter 1, your observations during classroom walk-throughs and discussion during the Teaching Adults session will already have provided you with at least a sense of each teacher's stage of concern regarding Knowledge of Students and Learning Community. A third data source can be collected immediately after each workshop by inviting teachers' written assessments of the workshop and including a question asking for teachers' concerns.

Learn More About the Concerns-Based Adoption Model

Hall, G. & Hord, S. (2001). *Implementing change: Patterns, principles, and potholes.* Boston, Massachusetts: Allyn & Bacon.

Each chapter moves from concept to application and includes research, case studies, discussion questions, and activities.

PROCESS: WORKSHOP ASSESSMENTS

3–5 minutes per Teaching Adults session

What Are They?

Workshop assessments are meaningful feedback about whether teachers feel they have acquired the knowledge, strategies, and skills being taught, as well as whether they found the session useful.

Steps in Creating Workshop Assessments

1. Identify the assessment's purpose. You might want to use the sample form (see BLM 3.2) each time so that you have a consistent measure of participants' reactions to the workshops. However, to determine participants' perceptions of their learning, you will need to identify the specific skills and content of each workshop and have participants rate their comfort with each, perhaps on a rubric, or, alternatively, you can have them respond to open-ended prompts such as "3 Positives and 1 Wish," "Cheers/Fears/Unclears," "Most Helpful/I Still Need," or "My concern about this work is _____."

2. Decide whether you need to be able to disaggregate responses based on characteristics of the participant, such as years of teaching experience, knowledge of the workshop topic, or grade level taught, or whether you have to know the identity of the respondent so you can provide individualized support. Note that this is not usually necessary (differentiation is based on flexible short-term groupings, not individualized programming) and also that you do not tend to get honest responses unless you can guarantee the anonymity of the respondents. See Q & A on page 45.

www.CartoonStock.com

3. Organize questions about participants' reactions into three categories (Guskey, 2000): workshop content, process (your facilitation and the activities), and context (the learning environment). By grouping the questions, participants will be able to focus on one aspect of the workshop at a time. Note that BLM 3.2 does not include questions on the learning environment. These are questions such as "Rate the quality of

the refreshments" and "Were the chairs comfortable?" They are important considerations and will have an impact on responses to other questions, but are not included here because your learning environment will likely stay fairly consistent over the course of the year. Once you have your workshop environment established and have confirmed with participants that it works, you do not need to keep asking if the chairs are comfortable and the coffee hot.

When Do You Do Them?

Ask teachers to complete assessments after each of your Teaching Adults sessions as well as after any other workshops or conferences held at your school or elsewhere.

Why Do Them?

- Teachers' indicators of satisfaction with the workshop informs your development of future sessions. You are therefore modelling the relationship between evidence and instruction.

- Teachers need to understand new instructional strategies and skills before they can implement them. Asking your teachers whether they have achieved this understanding tells you whether the workshop was effective and what you need to do to sustain the learning.

- By using the same assessment structure after each workshop, you or the session facilitator will have a better understanding of strengths and challenges as instructional leaders.

Who Does Them?

All teachers should complete workshop assessment forms.

> "The absence of accountability—knowing whether professional development made a difference, how much of a difference, and for whom—is the same as not caring whether it makes a difference."
>
> —Hayes Mizell

Q & A: Workshop Assessments

Q. I have a small staff, and I recognize most people's handwriting. How do I protect anonymity?

A. Don't ask questions that will result in identification of the individual, use rating scales rather than open-ended questions so that handwriting is unnecessary, and have someone other than yourself collect the completed forms.

Q. Some people find it easy to be critical. How I do help them recognize that their lack of effort and involvement might have something to do with their dissatisfaction with a workshop?

A. Tom Guskey suggests that your assessment form include a question in which participants can rate themselves as learners, because doing so often causes them to go back and change their responses to other questions. Here is the rating scale Guskey shares from Jay McTighe:

In this session I was a(n)
- ❏ non-learner
- ❏ semi-attentive
- ❏ engaged recipient
- ❏ active cooperator
- ❏ advanced synthesizer

Q. Who should be creating the workshop assessment form? Does it need to be the person facilitating the workshop?

A. As long as the individual(s) creating the assessment form have a good understanding of the goals of the session, anyone can create the form. If you are developing your plans with a team (see Chapter 4), the creation and management of assessment forms would be a good task for members of that team. Make sure that whoever is involved understands the importance of the assessment form, both for modelling useful assessments and for making decisions based on the data that is collected.

Peanuts: © United Feature Syndicate, Inc.

Q. Is one form of assessment better than another?

A. No; the format of the assessment should be determined according first to how the data will be used, and second to the time available to collect the information. Rating scores and rubric levels do not offer detailed information but are quick to complete and easy to collate. Open-ended questions provide helpful detail, but they are time-consuming for participants to complete and more difficult for you to collate and act on their advice. Many facilitators try for the best of both worlds by having a form with some rating scales and some open-ended questions, but this may not be successful if you are asking staff to complete the same form eight to ten times over the course of a school year.

Q. How do I get people to return their evaluation forms?

A. Make sure the forms are short and easy to complete. Stop the workshop a few minutes early to allow teachers enough time to complete the assessments before they have to leave. And, most importantly, make it explicit and obvious that you are using the assessment data to inform the development of the next workshop. Make sure to begin your next session with a quick, 30-second summary of something you learned from the assessment of the previous one and explain how you have altered the current workshop based on that learning.

Learn More About Evaluating Professional Learning

Guskey, T. (2000). *Evaluating professional development*. Thousand Oaks, California: Corwin Press.

Guskey's book has many useful suggestions for measuring the aspects of professional learning that contribute to improved student learning.

CHAPTER 4

Planning Professional Learning

CHAPTER AT A GLANCE

Section	Focus	Action/Time
Professional Learning (p. 47)	Characteristics of high-quality professional learning Reasons for whole-staff workshops Other forms of professional learning The role of teams	Read
Working with Data (p. 50)	Why you need data Establishing a goal Creating progress markers using Rapid Results	Read
Process (p. 54)	Creating a year or multi-year plan for professional learning about differentiated instruction	One or more meetings Duration determined by you

MODEL FOCUS

Entire Framework

Professional Learning

High-quality professional learning is

- sustained over time
- embedded in the daily work of the school and focused on school concerns
- based on student needs rather than teacher desires
- focused on specific content and/or instructional strategies for student achievement
- concerned with research-based best practices
- provided in a format that allows teachers to actively construct knowledge and reflect on learning rather than passively receive information
- evaluated to determine its impact and to guide next steps

And, as you might expect in this guide, high-quality professional learning is differentiated to meet the learning needs, interests, and preferences of individual teachers—to start where they are and provide the right level of appropriate challenge to advance their learning.

Facilitating or even arranging for the facilitation of consistently effective, high-quality professional learning sessions is a tall order but, as Thomas Guskey (2000, p. 3) suggests,

> . . . one constant finding in the research literature is that notable improvements in education almost never take place in the absence of professional development. At the core of each and every successful educational improvement effort is a thoughtfully conceived, well-designed, and well-supported professional development component.

Staff meetings dedicated to professional learning meet a number of the conditions of high-quality professional learning, providing a solid introduction to a concept or skill. Because they are intended for an entire staff, they also do an effective job of setting a school-wide goal, providing everyone with a common vocabulary, and creating or reinforcing common beliefs and values. It is difficult to ensure that everyone is even aware of a school focus if there is no venue for whole-staff learning. However, if you *only* offer monthly professional learning staff meetings with no follow-up and no opportunity for teachers to practise and receive feedback, you will not see the information presented in the staff room transferred to action in the classroom (Joyce and Showers, 2002).

A number of follow-up activities are suggested in the Sustain the Learning segments of the Teaching Adults lesson plans. For example, examining student work or writing assessments are logical next steps for teachers after attending a staff workshop about formative assessment. However, although this handbook offers suggestions for follow-up, try whenever possible to give teachers choice in how they practise and consolidate new learning. This acknowledges the adult learner's need for some ownership of the content of new learning, demonstrates respect for individual preferences, and is an easy way for people to self-differentiate.

There are a great many actions to sustain and extend the learning from a staff workshop. Here are two dozen examples. The first 15 come from a review of the table of contents in *Powerful Designs for Professional Learning* (Easton, 2004); the next nine come from a bookmark created by the National Staff Development Council.

[Sticky note: 24 Ways To Engage People In Professional Learning]

• Access student voices through interviews and focus groups.	• Engage in action research.	• Design and evaluate assessments with a colleague.
• Design curriculum/plan lessons with a colleague.		• Immerse in the experience as a learner.
• Keep a journal or reflective log.		• Be a mentor . . . or a mentee.
• Participate in peer coaching.		• Shadow students.
• Observe other teachers.		• Try visual dialogue.
• Analyze case studies.		• Teach others in your schools.
• Consult an expert.		• Write an article or give a conference presentation about your work.
• Read journals, educational magazines, or books.		• Participate in a critical friends group.

Sources: Adapted from Easton, 2004; National Staff Development Council.

Learn More About Professional Learning

Easton, L. B. (Ed.). (2004). *Powerful designs for professional learning.* Oxford, Ohio: National Staff Development Council.

Each powerful design is thoroughly introduced in ten pages of text, including rationale, steps in the process, critical elements, a list of resources for further information, and handouts on an accompanying CD-ROM.

Most powerful learning designs work to break the isolation of teachers in their individual classrooms. As noted educator Parker Palmer (1998) suggests, there are only two places a teacher can go to grow in his or her practice—within to reflection, or without to the community of fellow teachers. Collaborative teams—whether professional learning communities, critical friends groups, study groups, like-grade teams, or teams organized around choice of follow-up activity—provide essential support for the individuals engaged in the learning. If these learning communities or teams are not in place in your school, this will be a critical first step to sustaining the learning of your whole-staff workshops. If they are in place and if you ensure that team members have specific goals with timelines, that they have been taught collaborative processes such as how to solve problems or resolve conflicts (Conzemius and O'Neill, 2002), and that you stay involved with the team by sometimes sitting in on meetings, observing teachers in action, or requesting updates of progress, learning teams will be of tremendous value in sustaining and furthering your work on differentiated instruction or any other topic.

> "Teachers learn best by studying, doing, and reflecting; by collaborating with other teachers; by looking closely at students and their work; and by sharing what they see."
> —Linda Darling-Hammond

> "The growth of any craft depends on shared practice and honest dialogue among the people who do it.
> —Parker Palmer

Planning Professional Learning

Learn More About Supporting Teams

Conzemius, A., & O'Neill, J. (2002). *The handbook for SMART school teams.* Bloomington, Indiana: National Education Service (now Solution Tree).

This handbook and CD-ROM are an invaluable source of practical information on productive meetings, team growth and development, processes and planning tools for groups, and tools for evaluation.

Working with Data

Kouzes and Posner (1987) tell the story of two groups of soldiers participating in a 20-kilometre march. The first group is told exactly how far they have to go, and they are informed of their progress at several points along the way. The second group is simply told, "This is the long march you have been hearing about." Which group do you think fared better on the performance and stress tests administered at the end? The first group, by far. Which group is representative of teachers?

As school administrators and instructional leaders, we want to move our teachers away from the lethargic second group of soldiers toward the energetic first group who see the goal clearly and know how they are doing relative to its achievement. Therefore, we need to do two things:

1. Establish a clear and narrowly focused goal so that crossing the finish line is possible.

2. Set up progress markers along the way to keep people motivated and marching on the same path.

© The New Yorker Collection, 1973, Henry Martin from cartoonbank.com. All rights reserved.

Establish the Goal

In the process pages of this chapter, you are asked to establish an overall learning goal based on your review of existing data. There are four data measures to consider (Bernhardt, 2002):

- student learning (test scores, teacher observations, authentic assessments, and report cards)
- demographics (enrolment, attendance, ethnicity, gender, grade level, and native language)

> "Disaggregation is not a problem-solving activity; it's a problem-finding activity."
>
> —*Larry Lezotte*

- perceptions (the learning environment, values and beliefs, attitudes; perceptions of students, parents, and teachers)
- school processes (descriptions of programs, instructional strategies, classroom practices)

The more measures you are able to use in establishing your goal, the better. Using multiple measures will help you to disaggregate data so that your goal can be more precise. For example, if your review of student achievement and demographic data tells you that your boys' math scores start declining in Grade 3 and are in free fall by Grade 7, and your perception data confirms that boys detest math, it will be easy to write a clear and focused goal statement.

Learn More About Using Data in Goal-Setting

Bernhardt, V. (2004). *Data analysis for continuous school improvement* (2nd ed.). Larchmont, New York: Eye on Education.

Holcomb, E. (2001). *Asking the right questions: Techniques for collaboration and school change* (2nd ed.). Thousand Oaks, California: Corwin Press.

Holcomb, E. (2004). *Getting excited about data: Combining people, passion, and proof to maximize student achievement* (2nd ed.). Thousand Oaks, California: Corwin Press.

These books help administrators use data to determine where they are, where they want to be, and how to get there. Edie Holcomb's books are particularly useful for strategies that encourage staff collaboration in taking responsibility for all learners.

SET UP PROGRESS MARKERS

We all recognize that progress markers are necessary—teachers need to know they are making a positive difference to student achievement now, not ten years from now when a grateful student drops by with an invitation to their college graduation. The dilemma is in determining what data should be used to measure progress. We likely won't be able to use the same forms of data that we used in the establishment of our goal; that data may be the result of large-scale testing, attitude surveys administered yearly, and first-month enrolment reports administered near the beginning of the school year. Data of this kind is too far removed from teacher practice to have ongoing meaning and, of course, there are, or should be, limits to the number of times we test students.

I have had significant success across a number of schools using Mike Schmoker's "Rapid Results" structure (1999). The structure is simple. Teach the workshop—say, for example, one about the importance of teaching students how to summarize text. Ask teachers to simultaneously create a pre- and post-assessment of students' ability to summarize. The simultaneous creation is important because teachers will automatically make an assessment harder if they develop it after they have taught the strategy.

The assessments can be individual to each classroom and in any subject area. For example, a teacher might give students a geography selection they were going to be reading anyway and, without direction, ask students to write a summary of the selection. That is the pre-assessment, which the teacher reviews to determine who can summarize, who cannot, and what the teacher needs to do to further the learning in both cases. The teacher then teaches summarizing in whatever form he or she wishes. Near the end of the month, the teacher gives students a different geography selection, again says, "Please write a summary," and compares the two assessments. At the next workshop you ask, "How did your work on summarizing last month affect student learning? What evidence do you have to support your observation? Tell us what you did to get those results!"

Victoria Bernhardt says that school process data is the single most difficult measure to collect because teachers work intuitively and are too busy to reflect on and document their processes. That situation changes when using "Rapid Results." Staff will be reflecting on their processes, sharing ideas, planning next steps, and celebrating successes.

Learn More About Rapid Results

Schmoker, M. (1999). *Results: The key to continuous school improvement.* Alexandria, Virginia: ASCD.

PROCESS: Creating a Professional Learning Plan

 One or more meetings, duration to be determined by you

What Is It?

A professional learning plan is a tentative year-long or multi-year plan for a sequence of staff meeting workshops, with preliminary plans for follow-up activities to support and sustain the learning.

Who Is Involved?

Just as you should not be absent from instructional leadership, you should not own it. Planning the year with some or all of your teachers, or with teachers, parents, and other stakeholders if that is your process, simply makes good sense. Review your collaborative decision-making structures to see who should be involved. Is there a leadership team? A professional learning community or subgroup thereof? If you have a planning group already in place, it will likely work well as long as its members are representative of all divisions in the school. Ideally, however, your team should also include rookie teachers (either new to the profession or to the school) as well as the more experienced teachers, and, if possible, teachers who have some experience differentiating instruction as well as those who do not. Finally, if you include some resisters, not only will your plan be strengthened by their questions, but you will really make progress in implementation when you get them onside.

If you need to create a planning team, or if you are looking for additional members who might be able to assist with instruction in and beyond the staff meeting workshops, consider seeking teachers who meet Deborah Childs-Bowen's characteristics of teacher leaders (2006, p. 2). Look for teachers who:

- advocate for students
- accept responsibility for student performance and for the profession
- are open to learning and engaging in regular conversations about teaching and learning
- speak out about changes needed and provide plausible suggestions
- identify student, teacher, and school-wide needs
- inquire, reflect, and innovate
- deal with conflict without compromising goals or ideas

Steps in Planning

1. Meet with planning team members individually or as a group. Set dates for two planning sessions, perhaps a week apart, with each session lasting 60–90 minutes. You should be able to complete at least one full step of the planning process before the end of a meeting, or, more likely, several steps. Divide the staff amongst the planning team members and ask each member to speak with several individuals regarding the questions and concerns they have about differentiated instruction, their experience with differentiation, and the issue(s) they see as most significant in improving their students' achievement. You may want to involve team members in creating the interview questions or provide them with a form for recording the responses. Ask team members to write the responses in participants' own words wherever possible.

   (**Note:** If planning team members are identified prior to using the Chapter 1 lesson plan "What Is Differentiated Instruction?" you can set up table groups for that lesson so that team members are able to gather the data during the workshop and perhaps in a few extra minutes at the end. If that is the case, make sure you tell the entire staff what is happening and why.)

2. While some team members are gathering perception data, you and perhaps other team members are gathering relevant student achievement data and looking for a student need that is significant to all grades and that, when addressed, will have a demonstrable impact on student achievement. Refer to the four measures of data (pages 51–52) and decide what data you have that will be most helpful in determining your goal.

3. A clearly defined, collaboratively established goal will make all the difference in your ability to focus instruction for student achievement and to demonstrate that the goal has been achieved. Phrase the student achievement need as a SMART goal—specific, measurable, achievable, realistic, and timely. (For help with writing SMART goals, see Conzemius and O'Neill—either the *Handbook* mentioned earlier in this chapter or Chapter 5 of *Shared Responsibility* listed in the references.) Then try to break the goal down into a series of sub-goals or indicators that can be measured and observed throughout the year. Short-term successes are essential to maintaining staff energy and commitment and to determining if you are on the right track (Schmoker, 1999).

   Think carefully about the best way to engage in goal-setting in your school. Will you get buy-in only if all staff members are involved in reviewing the data and setting the goal? If so, you will need to have one or more additional meetings and you will need a collaborative process

> "If you cry 'Forward,' you must make clear the direction in which to go. Don't you see that if you fail to do that and simply call out the word to a monk and revolutionary, they will go in precisely the opposite directions."
>
> —*Anton Chekhov*

for determining the goal. Choosing an effective process will be dependent on your staff's prior experiences with collaboration (see references by Holcomb or Conzemius and O'Neill from this chapter for suggestions). If, on the other hand, you will be successful with a subgroup taking the goal forward to the planning meeting, this has the advantage of making you an equal partner in the meeting because you and the group have brought something for other team members to critique and improve.

4. Begin the planning meeting by sharing the proposed student achievement goal. Make a compelling case for addressing this goal by presenting the school data that indicates it is necessary, along with research or your reflections that speak to the significance of the goal to the curriculum and to a student's opportunity for success throughout life. Invite team members to compare the achievement goal to the individual priority issues identified by teachers, looking for points of connection. Team members can refine the student achievement goal by assessing it against the SMART acronym, and can review or create indicators and sub-goals.

5. Provide team members with a copy of BLM 4.1, which explains the *Success for Every Student* model and gives a few key indicators of beliefs and actions that would be evident in the classroom of a teacher who is both effective and differentiating for each component. Ask team members to individually read BLM 4.1 and, using both the questions and concerns they gathered in their informal interviews and their

knowledge of the overall student achievement goal, to prioritize each component for future workshops. Is the priority of each component an

→ A? (essential to success of the goal and reflective of colleagues' most significant questions and concerns)

→ B? (a bit less than A—important but not quite as essential and/or not a burning issue for colleagues)

→ C? (already mastered, not a burning issue for colleagues, or not as significant as other components)

6. After participants have had time to individually work through Step 4, use the "dotmocracy" process to quickly gather the information. List the components on a sheet of chart paper. Give each participant two colours of dot stickers—one for A priorities and one for B priorities—and ask them to prioritize the components listed on the chart using the stickers.

7. Tally the number of A and B priorities, inviting discussion for each. If there is a clear fit between model components and requirements necessary to successful goal achievement, refer to the appropriate chapters of this handbook for further information and to determine the number of workshop sessions and the number and nature of follow-up professional learning structures needed. Map these on to a calendar of staff meeting dates. Invite planning team members to volunteer or to suggest the names of staff who have experience, expertise, or interest in a topic and who would like to work on the development and presentation of a particular workshop.

If there is not a clear link between one or more model components and the requirements necessary to achieving your SMART goal, identify the problem. Is the goal too vague, uninspiring, or, for whatever reason, not supported by the team? Are the model components understood? Is there an overwhelming concern or question about differentiation that is going to be a barrier to progress unless it is addressed directly and immediately? Has the planning meeting simply gone on too long and people are too tired to make meaningful decisions? If you can clearly define the problem, you are more than half way to its solution.

8. Once a plan has been agreed on, write up the plan *and* represent it visually in a graphic organizer to demonstrate responsiveness to various learning preferences. Take some time before or during the next staff meeting date to share the learning plan with the staff and invite their responses, their offers of help, and their commitment to the plan.

9. Once agreed to by staff, keep the plan alive and the goal visible by posting it in a public place such as the staff room, and by referring frequently to it and to progress that is being made in its achievement.

> ## Q & A: Creating a Professional Learning Plan
>
> **Q. How long should this process take?**
>
> A. The length of time required to make the plan is dependent on whether you have all of the data needed to make good decisions, and whether you and your team have worked together before and have helpful processes in place for making decisions, resolving conflict, sharing a variety of viewpoints, and so on.
>
> The length of time required to implement the plan is dependent on whether achievement of the plan's goal will represent significant change for some or all of your staff and on your ability to work strategically based on each teacher's starting point.
>
> **Q. Speaking of change, where does CBAM fit into the planning?**
>
> A. You can use CBAM (see pages 39–40) as a pre-assessment of each individual's starting point after you have identified the priority components or, if you are having trouble determining the most important components (see Step 6 above), you can share BLM 4.1 with all staff members. Through discussion, classroom observation, or by sharing the CBAM structure directly, you can identify or have teachers self-identify their level on CBAM for each of the components being considered.
>
> **Q. Shouldn't I know more about my teachers' understanding before choosing the model components so that I can differentiate?**
>
> A. No; just as all students in a differentiated classroom have common essential understandings and learning goals, all teachers are working on the same overriding student achievement goal. Your current knowledge of staff, supported by planning team members' informal interview results, gives you the information you need to determine the model components that are going to be most important to achievement of that goal. Differentiation comes in *how* you teach the essential understandings and in how you support and sustain practice and consolidation of those understandings.

CHAPTER 5

Creating an Effective Learning Community

CHAPTER AT A GLANCE

Section	Focus	Action/Time
The Characteristics of a Learning Community (p. 59)	Characteristics Similarities across different communities Importance of community	Read
Your Role (p. 61)	The differences only an administrator can make in developing and sustaining learning communities	Read
Teaching Adults (p. 63)	Classroom management and organizational procedures that support differentiation	This session should be developed and facilitated by teachers. (See lesson plan for time requirements.)
Teaching Adults (p. 66)	The significance of a teacher's classroom presence; relationship to discipline and resiliency	30 minutes; no preparation required
Process (p. 69)	Encouraging reflection	Ongoing

MODEL FOCUS

Learning Community

The Characteristics of a Learning Community

When you drop in on a group of teachers at work together or participate in a committee meeting with teachers and parents, you know quite quickly whether the group is functioning as an effective learning community or if it is simply a number of individuals who are in the same space, at the same time, engaged in the same activity. Whether consciously aware of it or not, you register the presence or absence of some of the outward signs of an effective learning community: caring and generally friendly interactions, clearly established norms that allow and encourage productivity, trust as evidenced by a willingness to ask genuine questions, and, hopefully, a sense of excitement, energy, or enthusiasm for the work that is being done.

The advantages of an effective learning community to the individuals involved, to the school, and to society at large are positive and life-affirming. Compare, for example, the protective factors individuals need in order to be resilient to the actions demonstrated by individuals in a learning community:

To be resilient, individuals need (Benard, 2004)	In a learning community, individuals demonstrate (Sergiovanni, 1994)
• caring relationships	• care and concern for each other
• opportunities for participation and contribution	• responsibility for their own and each other's learning, and for the learning environment
• to use their strengths and interests as starting points for learning	• understanding and appreciation for the diversity of learners

"Your X-ray shows an enlarged heart. It's nothing to worry about. All teachers have a big heart."

www.CartoonStock.com

"If surgery and the law were practiced as privately as teaching, we would still treat most patients with leeches and dunk defendants in millponds."

—*Parker Palmer*

While we tend to focus on developing resiliency in our students, adults also need help dealing with the stresses and strains of work and life. Community offers this assistance by creating a shared sense of belonging and commitment to one another for all members.

Of course, effective learning communities, whether of students with their teacher or of adults together, cannot be built or sustained on warm feelings alone. They also need a goal—a clear collective purpose. In the classroom that goal is learning, which is demonstrated by various indicators of student achievement. For adults, the goal is also learning, as demonstrated by the dialogue that renders the private act of teaching public; that opens teaching and management practices to scrutiny. For the adult, the learning community "facilitates the exchange of ideas and the use of feedback to improve professional practices" (Martin-Kniep, 2004, p. 2). Community encourages and supports a collaborative rather than an individualized or balkanized school staff.

Individualistic (resent intrusion of others)	**Balkanized** (small groups aligned against others)	**Contrived Collegiality** (together, but not focused on teaching and learning)	**Collaborative** (working together to improve teaching and management strategies)

Source: Fullan and Hargreaves, 1996.

Learn More About Adult Learning Communities

Shirley Hord, one of the authors of CBAM (see Chapter 3, page 39), developed the term "professional learning community" (Blankstein, 2004, p. 55); however, the authors who are best known for their extensive work in this field are Richard DuFour, Robert Eaker, and Rebecca DuFour.

DuFour, R. & Eaker, R. (1998). *Professional learning communities at work.* Bloomington, Indiana: National Education Service.

Eaker, R., DuFour, R., & DuFour, R. (2002). *Getting started: Reculturing schools to become professional learning communities.* Bloomington, Indiana: National Education Service.

Your Role

There are a number of supports for both adult learning communities and classroom communities that either require your involvement or that only you can provide. These supports—time, challenging goals, and rules of behaviour—are explored in the table below.

Necessary to Community	To Support the Adult Learning Community	To Support the Classroom Learning Community
Time	Create time for teachers to work together. For example: • timetable common preparation times for like-grade teachers • turn staff meetings into professional learning workshops • occasionally hire substitute teachers to allow you to release a number of staff to work together	Protect instructional time by: • reducing interruptions, such as announcements, that take attention away from learning • timetabling so that movement of students and number of teachers in contact with a student are minimized
Challenging Goals	Establish challenging school-wide achievement goals to provide a focus for learning-community work	Encourage teachers to work with students to create class goals that emerge from the school-wide goals, and individual goals related to the class goals

Necessary to Community	To Support the Adult Learning Community	To Support the Classroom Learning Community
Rules of Behaviour	Help teams create protocols for, among others: • decision-making • managing meetings • sharing workload • commitment (i.e., attendance) • monitoring progress • resolving conflict • reporting results	Establish and enforce a school-wide behaviour policy so that behavioural expectations outside of the classroom are consistent with expectations within the classroom

If you are familiar with Robert Marzano's (2003) summary of school effectiveness research, you may have recognized these necessities of community as concepts embedded in his descriptions of school-level factors that have been proven to have a significant, demonstrable, and positive impact on student achievement. By paying attention to community at the levels of both classroom and school, you will have an impact not just on students, but also on adult achievement and satisfaction.

Learn More About Finding Time for Learning

There aren't any easy answers to finding time for the adults in your school to work together, but the Spring 2007 issue of *Journal of Staff Development* (volume 28, issue 2) is built around the theme of time management and is a good place to start crafting your own unique solutions.

TEACHING Adults

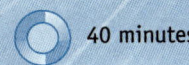

40 minutes

Classroom Management and Organizational Procedures That Support Differentiation

Significance to student achievement	Abraham Maslow's hierarchy of needs has withstood the test of time. Created more than 50 years ago, the hierarchy indicates that the human need for belonging or group affiliation must be met before we can expect to address questions of self-esteem or self-actualization. The bottom line is that classrooms need to be emotionally safe before students can focus on academics.
Common questions and issues	• If I am not well organized, does that mean I won't be able to differentiate effectively? • How do I get my students to be responsible for their own learning?
When would you use this lesson?	Since an effective classroom community is an essential precursor to differentiated instruction, this session, if needed at all, should be provided early in the school year. An ideal time would be immediately following an end-of-September parent–teacher evening (see Teach the Session, below).
Materials you need	• Work Kit (1 per group) • BLM 5.2 Classroom Procedures That Support Differentiation (1 per person, plus some extras) • BLM 3.2 Workshop Assessment (1 per person, modified for this workshop)
Suggested group set-up	Teacher choice

Creating an Effective Learning Community   63

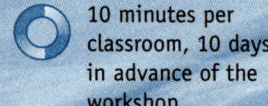

10 minutes per classroom, 10 days in advance of the workshop

Build the Evidence Base

The purpose of this session is to have all teachers leave the workshop with ideas for effective procedures and classroom organization that facilitate students taking responsibility and sharing ownership of the classroom. Such conditions increase the chance for differentiated instruction to succeed and not be sabotaged by classroom management concerns.

Although there are many good suggestions available in a number of books, organizational strategies are best learned close to home, where they can be viewed in action, practised, and supported. They should be taught by teachers who are effective classroom managers. Therefore, for this particular session, Build the Evidence Base preparation time is devoted to finding the positive examples that are in your school and deciding how they will be highlighted in the workshop and who will highlight them. To find positive examples, consider the information provided on BLM 5.1 (Management Procedures for a Differentiated Classroom) and look for these examples, or others, within your school.

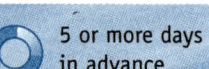

5 or more days in advance

Teach the Session

Teachers are given a copy of BLM 5.2 (Classroom Procedures That Support Differentiation) and are asked to complete it.

Workshop facilitators will have decided the best way of having participants complete BLM 5.2. Two possibilities beyond a standard workshop are the following:

- create a school-wide scavenger hunt
- take digital photographs and do a workshop slide show, with teachers speaking about their photographs

Timing matters if either of these options are chosen. Hold the workshops very close to the beginning of your parent–teacher night since all classrooms will be looking their best at that time.

Sustain the Learning

Students should be able to move around a room without falling over people or things. If they cannot, host your own version of a TV reality show in which spaces are purged and reclaimed.

Release one of your highly organized teachers to consult with a colleague who requests assistance. Provide a small budget for plastic bins, coloured file folders, or whatever else the highly organized and the organized-in-training teachers agree is necessary.

Determine an area of interest or need for optional workshops, advanced study, or action research projects. Some possibilities include creating a classroom library, organizing choices you provide to students, classroom jobs students can do, running effective class meetings or community circles, or creating classroom agreements.

TEACHING Adults

Teacher Presence

30 minutes

Significance to student achievement	This session focuses on the role of the teacher in forging a connection with every student and in creating a caring and emotionally safe environment. Students need to feel they belong before they can attend to academics.
Common questions and issues	• How can I respond to negative behaviours I don't even see? • My students are mean to each other. I don't think there's much I can do about it; that's just the way some classes are.
When would you use this lesson?	This workshop may be used at any time during the school year, but you may particularly wish to offer it when teachers need to be reminded that they are doing a good job and playing an important role in their students' lives.
Materials you need	• Work Kit (1 per group) • Blank paper—large enough to accommodate outlines of a teacher's hands (1 sheet per person) • Art supplies—beyond what is available in work kits (e.g., pastels, pencil crayons, watercolour paints, glitter, stickers) • Refreshments—perhaps something special such as a cake
Suggested group set-up	Teacher choice

Build the Evidence Base

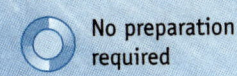
No preparation required

This session is about "withitness" and emotional objectivity. You already know which teachers are effective classroom managers and which ones struggle. This workshop is intended to acknowledge the former and give subtle but helpful support to the latter.

Teach the Session

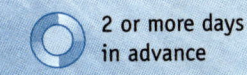
2 or more days in advance

Welcome teachers. Talk about their significance to the students in their classrooms, to parents, to you, to the school community at large. Give specific examples.

Say that this workshop is intended as a short refresher and an acknowledgment of the myriad ways in which they have a positive impact on their students every day. Ask teachers to work with a partner and trace an outline of each other's hands (activity adapted from Chapman & King, 2005, p. 21). Both hands should be traced on a single sheet of paper; the hands can be arranged in any position the person wishes.

When this has been done, talk about the concept of "withitness." Teachers will likely remember having heard of this concept in faculty of education classes on management. Agree that withitness was indeed first coined by Jacob Kounin to describe teachers who seem, according to their students, to have eyes in the back of their heads. In this definition, withitness is mainly a proactive discipline strategy.

Say that you would like to extend the definition of withitness to include all of the meaningful ways that teachers demonstrate care and encourage shared classroom ownership in their daily interactions with students. Give examples, such as class meetings, having spontaneous conversations with students about their interests, greeting students at the door of the room, establishing clear boundaries that set out which comments are acceptable and which are not, and so on. Ask each teacher to quickly jot down at least six ways they demonstrate withitness in their classroom. They can do their writing on the sheet of drawing paper outside of the hands.

Ask teachers to do a round robin small group share of one of their six comments, then to do a second sharing in response to the prompt, "A time when my best efforts at withitness didn't work." Stress that the second sharing is intended to reassure us that we all have less-than-stellar moments; group members should not give advice unless it is specifically requested.

Have teachers take the remaining workshop time to have fun decorating the inside of their hands with words, images, and colours that represent their classroom withitness. Hands can be cut out and displayed or kept by teachers as reminders of the great work they do each and every day.

Sustain the Learning

Teachers who struggle with classroom management may benefit from observing another teacher. Since effective management techniques may not be obvious to a teacher who does not know what to look for, observations should be conducted with a peer coach or consultant who can help the teacher recognize and interpret the effective practices that are being demonstrated. Left alone, we tend to see only what we expect to see.

Teachers who would like to self-assess their withitness quotient might refer to the self-assessment in Chapter 5 of the professional book *Start Where They Are: Differentiating for Success with the Young Adolescent*. The withitness assessment, like many of the structures and practices in the book, is applicable to all grade levels.

PROCESS: ENCOURAGING REFLECTION

○ Ongoing

What Is It?

Reflection comprises a number of different processes that encourage and support teachers in thinking and talking about their teaching practices. The purpose of reflection is to examine the impact of those practices on student achievement.

When Do You Encourage Reflection?

Encouraging reflection says that you believe that the adults in a school are and should be learners just as much as the students. Teachers should see you as a person who always asks probing questions that encourage examination of practice—theirs and yours.

Why Do It?

Taking time to reflect allows teachers to

- pause so they don't end up regretting decisions made in the heat of a disciplinary moment with students
- develop their understanding of how to improve their teaching in order to maximize student learning
- be aware of their learning
- have a better understanding of their beliefs and motivations
- deepen their understanding of how to teach students to be reflective, metacognitive learners
- model reflection for students

> "Follow effective action with quiet reflection. From the quiet reflection will come even more effective action."
> —*James Levin*

Who Does It?

Parker Palmer (1998, p. 160) says, "Good talk about good teaching can take many forms and involve many conversation partners—and it can transform teaching and learning. But it will happen only if leaders expect it, invite it, and provide hospitable space for the conversation to occur." Teachers will be responsible for the reflecting. Your role as administrator is to expect, invite, encourage, model, mentor, and probe.

Creating an Effective Learning Community

Ways to Encourage Reflection

Learning communities of all forms are built around reflection. Teachers consider and discuss the details of their teaching.

Reflective conversations are dialogues focused on teaching practices and how they can be improved. They are carefully structured to avoid the two extreme positions of not responding to someone's concern or of jumping in to fix or rescue the individual.

Reflective questions could be considered mini versions of the reflective conversation. They are questions that are typically asked by an administrator, although not necessarily. A favourite reflective question, apparently asked by Ralph Waldo Emerson whenever he met up with someone he hadn't seen for a while, was "What has become more clear to you since last we met?" Or, in slightly less formal terms, "What have you learned this week?"

Journals can be private or public. In both forums, their aim is to promote reflectiveness; that is, they need to include more than a description of events. Killion (2004, p. 127 in Easton) suggests that ideal journal entries also include "the teacher's response to the event, an analysis of the event in relationship to education research or theory, and a generalization or learning from the experience." If you want to use journals as a structured reflective tool, see Killion's chapter in *Powerful Designs for Professional Learning*.

Q & A: ENCOURAGING REFLECTION

Q: Is it really possible to teach reflection? Aren't some people simply more reflective than others?

A: Learning preferences research, including multiple intelligences theory, confirms that some people are more reflective than others and you may not be able to directly teach reflection and expect it to "take." However, reflectiveness is so important to improving teaching and learning that you should make deliberate efforts to ask reflective questions of individuals who don't tend to do that for themselves. Make questions quite specific at first—What worked in this activity? Why do you think it worked so well? What didn't work? Why not? You may never get to Emerson's "What has become more clear to you since last we met?" with some people, but encouraging reflection through any means will reap dividends for all.

CHAPTER 6

Knowing Your Learners

CHAPTER AT A GLANCE

Section	Focus	Action/Time
The Strengths Revolution (p. 71)	Making a focus on strengths part of your school's culture	Read
Process (p. 75)	Acknowledging staff strengths	Ten minutes per person, at least once per term
Teaching Adults (p. 77)	Individual differences in learners Sense-based learning styles DI structure—using a choice board	40–50 minutes, plus 30–45 minutes of optional preparation
Teaching Adults (p. 82)	Multiple intelligences	40 minutes, plus 0–30 minutes of preparation
Teaching Adults (p. 87)	Student interests	30 minutes; prepared by teachers

MODEL FOCUS

Knowledge of Students
Knowledge of Teachers

The Strengths Revolution

In a similar vein to the "tree falling in the forest" puzzle that is a favourite of first-year philosophy students everywhere, researcher, author, and speaker Marcus Buckingham might be asking himself, "If I announce that something is a revolution and no one pays any attention, is it still a revolution?"

Buckingham, with colleagues Donald Clifton and Curt Coffman, tried to start a revolution in management and leadership circles. In their work at the Gallup organization, they reviewed 5 million pages of transcript representing

> "Glance at problems, gaze at strengths."
>
> —*Unknown*

90-minute interviews with 80 000 managers. Their goal was to determine the distinguishing characteristics of particularly effective managers running highly successful divisions within otherwise ordinary companies. To achieve this, they asked a number of questions. When all of the data was analyzed, a core set of 12 questions proved to measure the strength of a workplace and, of these questions, six had the strongest links to the most outcomes. The six questions are (Buckingham and Coffman, 1999, p. 28):

- Do I know what is expected of me at work?
- Do I have the materials and equipment I need to do my work right?
- At work, do I have the opportunity to do what I do best every day?
- In the last seven days, have I received recognition or praise for doing good work?
- Does my supervisor, or someone at work, seem to care about me as a person?
- Is there someone at work who encourages my development?

Expecting a shopping list—a hit parade of the top 20 characteristics in response to the six core questions—Buckingham and Coffman were amazed to discover that great managers had only one thing in common: they all recognized the strengths of the individuals they worked with and, whenever and wherever possible, focused more on building and furthering those strengths than they did on identifying and remediating weaknesses.

It is an idea that seems too simple to be revolutionary, and too revolutionary to be possible. Many of us might think that it is a fine concept for the business world where people can take on specialized roles, but that a focus on strengths could not possibly work in education. After all, our students are young and need to develop strengths in all areas; teachers had best be strong in all aspects of teaching; and administrators, well, administrators clearly have to be good at everything—including instructional leadership.

Yet, we have hopefully all had times in our lives when we were in the state that Csikszentmihalyi calls "flow"—that period of time when our strengths perfectly matched the challenges of the task and we felt powerful, capable, completely in control of the work yet challenged by it, oblivious to time. It is exciting to imagine the energized and positive climate of a school community in which more of its members experience "flow" more of the time, or at least where all members know and value their strengths, and where they have regular opportunities to use them.

A strengths revolution in our schools would not, of course, be starting from zero. Although circumstances beyond our control sometimes mean that teachers have to teach in a discipline or a grade level where they don't feel especially confident or which they do not enjoy, we try our best to match teachers with their subject and grade preferences. We give teachers who are passionate about a particular subject area as many classes in that subject as possible without creating timetables in which students see a different teacher every 30 or 40 minutes and lose their connection to a single, meaningful adult. Every spring at placement meetings we endeavour, however imprecisely, to match teacher and student personalities or teaching styles and learning preferences. What more can we do?

I propose that the revolution in our schools will come when we shift our thinking, not our activity. Can you identify a half-dozen strengths of every member of your staff? Do they know you are aware of these strengths? Are there times when they are called upon to use their strengths, even if they are not the obvious ones like the ability of the music or drama teacher to mount a production, or the physical education teacher to coach teams? The Process section in this chapter encourages you to identify and acknowledge staff strengths using simple observations you make of teachers' daily work. In doing so, the belief and hope is that when teachers experience the positive benefits of having their strengths recognized, they, in turn, will shift more of their attention to recognizing and developing their students' strengths.

The focus on strengths is easier for administrators with teachers than it is for teachers with students. An old joke claims that there are two kinds of people in the world: those who believe that everything can be divided into two categories, and everyone else. It is human nature to think of the world in terms of contrast: good/evil, hero/villain, left/right, logic/emotion, strength/weakness. Many teachers believe that they have not earned their salary if they are not focused on eradicating student weaknesses. The problem is that in the process, strengths are too often shoved to the side, either unacknowledged or considered unimportant. Further, a focus on weaknesses leads to some highly ineffective teaching practices, such as the use of unimaginative, limiting worksheets that chop sophisticated skills like reading into bits of meaningless drill.

CALVIN AND HOBBES © 1993 Watterson. Dist. by UNIVERSAL PRESS SYNDICATE. Reprinted with permission. All rights reserved.

Acknowledging and working from student strengths is an important part of knowing the learner, which is, of course, vital to differentiating instruction. It does not mean that weaknesses are ignored or never addressed, but rather that equal time is given to strengths. The rationale for this approach, along with specific information about how to teach it, is provided in the three Teaching Adults sessions in this chapter. As is true of each of chapters 5 to 11, each Teaching Adults session stands alone so that you can use any or all of them, in any order, and at any time of the year, depending on staff needs and your differentiated instruction goals.

Learn More About the Strengths Revolution

This book summarizes the strengths research:

Buckingham, M. & Coffman, C. (1999). *First, break all the rules: What the world's greatest managers do differently.* New York: Simon & Schuster.

This book reviews Gallup's strengths language. A code is provided so you can take the strengths-finder assessment online:

Buckingham, M. & Clifton, D. (2001). *Now, discover your strengths.* New York: Free Press, a division of Simon & Schuster.

If you would like to examine the idea of strengths from multiple perspectives, including marriage:

Buckingham, M. (2005). *The one thing you need to know . . . about great managing, great leading, and sustained individual success.* New York: Free Press, a division of Simon & Schuster.

If you want strengths language interpreted for teachers:

Liesveld, R., & Miller, J. (2005). *Teach with your strengths: How great teachers inspire their students.* New York: Gallup Press.

For a fascinating and inexpensive discussion and demonstration by Marcus Buckingham, use a search engine to locate Marcus Buckingham on the internet and buy his six short films in a two-DVD set entitled *Trombone Player Wanted* (2007).

PROCESS: ACKNOWLEDGING STAFF STRENGTHS

10 minutes per person, at least once a term

What Is It?

Written or verbal acknowledgment of one or more strengths, with specific evidence to support and, where possible, an opportunity for the staff member to make use of this strength in his or her work.

Why Do It?

- It is human nature to want to be acknowledged for our strengths.
- Acknowledging strengths makes your school culture more positive and optimistic.
- We want teachers to acknowledge student strengths and support them through a variety of instructional approaches. Acknowledging teachers for their strengths is akin to having them put on their oxygen mask first so they can help others.

"Man, how did they ever catch you?"

Who Does It?

One of the pleasures of leadership is acknowledging and inspiring the people who work with you. If you are a leader with formal authority, such as an administrator, there is no question that you should acknowledge strengths, both in writing and verbally. If your authority is informal, as in the case of coaches, consultants, and teacher leaders (including members of school leadership teams), you will need to determine whether written acknowledgments of your colleagues will be well received. Sincere verbal acknowledgments are always appreciated.

When Do You Do It?

Provide a written acknowledgment of a strength once per term, and a verbal acknowledgment whenever you can. Written acknowledgments are more genuine and easier to write if you deliberately set out to notice strengths, but spread your effort over a number of days or weeks so the arrival of your card in a teacher's mailbox is unpredictable. Knowing that everyone is getting a note from the principal today, or even this week, makes it look as if you have

TIME MANAGEMENT TIP

Buy boxes of notecards so you always have them on hand. Determine how many cards you are going to write each week. If Friday rolls around and you haven't met your quota, stay a few extra minutes and get them done. If you've had a particularly tough week and just can't write one more word, leave a verbal message on the staff member's home answering machine. It will be a pleasant surprise when they arrive home.

checked another task off your to-do list rather than sincerely noticing a strength and caring enough to acknowledge it.

Steps in Acknowledging Staff Strengths

1. Refer to BLM 6.1 for a variety of descriptors and corresponding labels for strengths you may notice in your staff. Please note that these terms are the author's, not those used by the Gallup organization. Those terms are available only through the resources listed in Learn More About, page 74. While the books are well worth reading, the value of this process is in your noticing strengths and acknowledging them. Feel free to add additional strengths and to substitute any language that works for you.

2. As you read the various strengths descriptors, names of staff will immediately come to mind as perfect examples of a given strength. Keep a staff list beside you as you review BLM 6.1 and note appropriate strengths beside each name. See the Q & A below for what to do when you can't identify a strength for a staff member.

TIME MANAGEMENT TIP

It can take a bit of time to turn your mind to the language of appreciation. Once in that mindset, you will save time if you write cards to two or three people, or separate cards to a single person. If you don't date the cards, you can save them for presentation at opportune moments.

3. Acknowledgment notes are a form of feedback, and good feedback always provides specific evidence. If you can write the note with telling details in place, great. If not, take a few minutes to gather the details. A quick walk-through of the teacher's classroom, a casual well-placed question, or a review of paperwork usually does the trick.

Q & A: ACKNOWLEDGING STAFF STRENGTHS

Q. I feel terrible admitting it, but there is one person on my staff that I really don't like. I can't think of a single strength this person possesses. I don't want to be dishonest. Should I just skip acknowledging this person?

A. No, this is an occasion for you to seek and find, not ignore. Review the strengths list (BLM 6.1), observe this person in action, have casual conversations with their friends—do whatever it takes to find the individual's strengths and focus on them. After all, that is what you are asking teachers to do with their students.

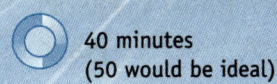

TEACHING Adults

40 minutes
(50 would be ideal)

Introduction to Individual Differences and Sense-Based Learning Styles

Significance to student achievement	In this lesson, the focus is first on identifying the aspects of an individual that affect schooling and that teachers can influence, and second on meeting the needs and preferences of kinesthetic and tactile learners. When their needs are not addressed, these learners often disengage and may become classroom, and eventually office, discipline problems. Achievement concerns are sidelined, not just for the individual, but sometimes for the class.
Common questions and issues	• Teachers may feel that in order to teach successfully, they must behave as if the students in their class are more alike than different, whereas the reverse is the reality. • The majority of teachers are visual and/or auditory learners. They do not know how to support kinesthetic learners, and may not recognize or value the learning that results.
When would you use this lesson?	If you are planning to teach more than one "Knowing Your Learners" workshop, you may want to use this one first. It is an introduction to individual differences. Learning styles are easier for teachers to observe than are multiple intelligences, and they are more practical in classroom application than student interests.
Materials you need	• Work Kit—1 per group • BLM 6.2 Ways Individuals Differ—cards to sort (one set per group or per pair) • BLM 6.3 Categories of Differences—category sort (1 per person, including you) • BLM 6.4 Choice Board (1 per group, or photocopy onto back of BLM 6.3 for 1 per person) • Several sheets of flipchart paper • BLM 3.2 Workshop Assessment (1 per person, modified for this workshop)

Knowing Your Learners 77

Suggested group set-up	Create cross-grade groupings with representatives of visual, auditory, and kinesthetic teaching in each group (see Build the Evidence Base). If you did not do the work to build your evidence base, simply create cross-grade groupings.
	Signify each table according to a colour or letter. You can then post a corresponding list or hand out colour or letter tags as staff arrive at the workshop.

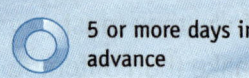 5 or more days in advance

Build the Evidence Base

Use this lesson to encourage or to reinforce teaching that is varied to meet the needs of visual, auditory, and kinesthetic learners. Determining the current state of affairs involves you walking the halls of your school and glancing in each classroom. That will give you a sense of the dominant learning style in play *at that moment in time.* Since some subjects are obviously taught more through one style than another (e.g., physical education is almost exclusively kinesthetic), you will need to repeat this process at different times of the day and on different days of the week in order to get an accurate picture of whether all sense-based learning styles are being regularly addressed in each classroom.

Note the approach as...	If the students are mostly...
visual	reading or viewing videos or overhead transparencies
auditory	listening to the teacher or to a recording
tactile/kinesthetic	experiencing—dramatizing, playing games, demonstrating, using manipulatives, drawing, painting, and so on

Make up a simple chart as shown. List teachers' names in order of the classrooms that you pass as you walk the school in a given pattern. Jot the first letter of the dominant sense at the moment in time you observe. If you want more detail than the standard three of Visual/Auditory/Kinesthetic (VAK), separate reading from visual (VARK) or tactile from kinesthetic (VACT). Note that using

78 Chapter 6

a pen or pencil to complete a worksheet does not qualify as a tactile activity! List seatwork as such, or as visual/auditory.

Day & Time Name	Mon. 9:15	Tues. 2:00	Wed. 10:30	Thurs. 1:00	Fri. 11:20
Sarah	K	V	V	K	K
Jeff	A	K	V	A	K
Joe	A	A	A	A	A
Denise	A	V	K	A	V

If you have taken a number of samplings over an extended period of time and see lots of variation, you probably do not need to bother with this workshop, even as a reinforcer. If, however, your review shows that teachers are favouring one learning style, proceed with the lesson. If your school conforms to research findings, you may find that teachers have increasing difficulty supporting kinesthetic learners as students advance through the grades and the subject matter becomes more abstract. In that case, you may opt to work with those teachers in a divisional, rather than whole-staff, meeting.

Do not share the results of this first evidence-gathering session with teachers. You have only sampled over a single week, and what you have seen is likely influenced by the content that is being taught and even the time of year. The results of your week of walks are intended to help you determine two things: 1) whether the workshop is needed and, if so, for whom; and 2) to allow you to refine your workshop content so that it addresses the specific needs of your staff. Although it is most likely the kinesthetic learners that receive short shrift in a school, it could be any group. Knowing the particulars for your school allows you to differentiate your workshop content.

Teach the Session

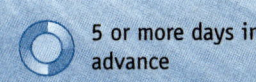
5 or more days in advance

Teachers arrive and sit at tables organized according to the suggested group set-up. Ask teachers to number off within their group (1–4 or 1–6 depending on group size) and to remember their number.

Give each group a set of cards (BLM 6.2). Alternatively, to increase the number of people handling the cards, you can give a set to each pair within a group and have them compare their results with others at their table in order to arrive at a group response.

Tell them that the cards represent all of the ways that one student may differ from another. Ask them to read through the cards and to set aside any differences that teachers cannot address or can afford to ignore in their planning and instruction. Limit groups to a few minutes to do this task, then choose a number (1–4 or 1–6 depending on group size) and have the group member with that number report the group's decisions and rationale to the staff. You should hear that there are many aspects of an individual student that influence their schooling. Record any individual differences that teachers feel they cannot or do not need to address on the flipchart. If there is general agreement, have each group set those cards aside.

Next, ask each teacher to complete BLM 6.3, where they will sort the cards into three categories, leaving category headings to their choice or predetermining the headings. If you would like this activity to be a self-assessment, you could create headings along the lines of "Use in my classroom," "Would like to know more," and "Not a priority." As teachers complete the worksheet, note who uses the cards to do their sorting (tactile) and who does the work in discussion with others rather than alone (auditory).

Give each group a choice board (BLM 6.4) or photocopy it for each individual on the back of BLM 6.3, and ask them to complete their choice of task (one from the first row of the board, and one from the second). If you have kept the activities moving, you should still have at least 20 minutes left in the workshop. Advise teachers that they will only have ten minutes to do as much of the activity as they can, since the last ten minutes will be devoted to sharing ideas. Say that you would like each teacher to be able to leave the session with one new idea for addressing an individual difference in their classroom.

While teachers are working, use a copy of BLM 6.3 to divide teachers into three categories according to whether their choice of activity is predominantly visual, auditory, or kinesthetic. You will know this by referring to the second row of the choice board that has activities organized in VAK order, and by the notes you made from the previous activity.

Put workshop assessment forms on tables; some teachers may want to complete them early.

Call staff back together for the final ten minutes of the workshop, and repeat your desire that everyone leave with a new idea for addressing an individual difference in their classroom. Mention that the choice board they used is an example of a differentiation structure that is easy to develop and that honours student choice, a key principle of a differentiated classroom. It is also a simple way for students to select activities that match their learning styles. Point out or ask teachers to identify that the first column in the second row offers activities for visual learners, the second for auditory, and the third for tactile/kinesthetic. Note that there are inventories students can complete to determine their preferred style (one is available in *Start Where They Are*), but that simply providing the range of activities and observing individuals' selections gave you some quick insight into the teachers' preferences and that the same will be true for teachers with their students.

Invite teachers to share any activities that they were able to complete. If they didn't have time to complete the activity, they should each be able to share an idea related to the topic they chose. If your staff is large or if the activities are lengthy or elaborate, you may need to break into smaller groups for sharing or agree to run the workshop beyond the stated end time.

Thank teachers for attending the workshop and for sharing their ideas in lively and interesting ways. Ask them to complete the workshop assessment if they haven't already done so.

Sustain the Learning

Check in with teachers over the next couple of weeks, asking them if there was an idea from the workshop that they thought had merit and, if they tried it, how it worked for them in their classroom. Try to cross-pollinate ideas, encouraging one teacher to touch base with another. Not only is this a good way to build connections across the grades, but it makes obvious your interest in teachers trying new actions as a result of the workshop.

TEACHING Adults

MULTIPLE INTELLIGENCES

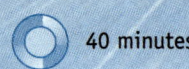 40 minutes

Significance to student achievement	Multiple intelligences are the *formats* in which our minds think. Robert Sternberg (2006, pp. 33–34), who developed the triarchic intelligence model, conducted an experiment in which he found that "when we teach students in a way that fits how they think, they do better in school. Students with creative or practical abilities, who are almost never taught or assessed in a way that matches their pattern of abilities, may be at a disadvantage in course after course, year after year."
Common questions and issues	• Not all concepts can be taught in eight different ways. How am I supposed to make this work? • Are learning centres the only way to use multiple intelligences? • I have no idea how to help my bodily kinesthetic or naturalist kids.
When would you use this lesson?	You could use this lesson with your entire staff at any point during the year. However, entry points, the focus of this session, are helpful only when teachers have made sure the material they are teaching is worth the effort and they have identified essential understandings and questions. Please review the two Teaching Adults sessions in Chapter 7 to determine if you need to teach them first.
Materials you need	• "Multiple Intelligences" PowerPoint presentation and necessary equipment • Work Kit (1 per group) • Sheet of flipchart paper or access to whiteboard; markers • BLM 6.5 Multiple Entry Points (1 per person) • Six-sided dice—(1 per grade or subject partners plus a few extra) • BLM 3.2 Workshop Assessment (1 per person, modified for this session)
Suggested group set-up	If teachers plan with grade or subject partners, ask them to sit with those individuals.

Build the Evidence Base

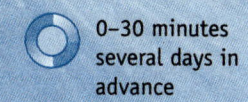
0–30 minutes several days in advance

In this session, you will be encouraging teachers to make use of multiple entry points to learning in order to meet the varying preferences of the learners in their classrooms. Although all or most teachers will already be familiar with the concept of multiple intelligences and can probably recite Howard Gardner's eight ways of being smart, it is likely that they experimented with intelligence-based learning centres after attending a workshop on the topic and then abandoned the effort because it proved onerous and of questionable value.

Because this session gives teachers new information about multiple intelligences that will allow them to apply the theory more effectively in their classrooms, it is of value to all teachers regardless of their prior experience with the concept. Therefore, it is not necessary that you build an evidence base to determine that the session will be useful. However, if you would like to collect baseline data or even simply to get teachers thinking about the upcoming session, ask (or have members of the planning team ask) teachers if they give multiple intelligences inventories to their students, how they make use of the results of those inventories, and what their experiences have been with multiple intelligences in the past.

Teach the Session

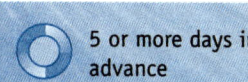
5 or more days in advance

Have this slide projected as teachers enter the room so they can be discussing the topic rather than waiting for the workshop to begin. Invite responses, helping teachers come to the understanding that learning styles are about how we prefer to receive, process, and analyze information, while intelligences are the formats we use for thinking.

PPT 6.1

Say that Howard Gardner's contribution to the world was the letter "s" (adding "s" to the word "intelligence"). Explain a little bit about his work—that he is a cognitive psychologist from Harvard University who developed his theory a couple of dozen years ago with the intention of engaging other cognitive psychologists in a discussion of how the mind works. Say that Robert Sternberg is a contemporary of Gardner's and that he also developed a theory of mul-

PPT 6.2

tiple intelligences, although in his case he posits three intelligences—practical, creative, analytic—where Gardner suggests eight or nine. Indicate that despite the fact that Sternberg's work might be easier to manage because there are fewer intelligences, teachers everywhere have embraced Gardner's work and have done their best to make use of it in the classroom.

Invite teachers to tell you Gardner's eight or nine intelligences, and jot them down on a board or flipchart paper. Review the list and ask teachers if they have had much success implementing these intelligences. Teachers who have can share how they do it; teachers who haven't will appreciate your reassurance that Howard Gardner never intended that we should try to teach a single concept in eight or nine different ways.

Explain that in recent writings, Howard Gardner has offered some clarifications that will make our teaching lives much easier and our work with multiple intelligences theory more effective.

Multiple clicks will build this slide. Read or say the following explanations as you put each term on the screen:

Potentials

The first realization is to understand that when our students complete multiple intelligences inventories, they are not telling us what they are good at, but only what they think they prefer. We cannot determine a student's intelligences through their preferences; we have to set up situations in which they can make use of different intelligences and observe them in action.

Profiles

Our second realization is that it is useful to think of student preferences in terms of a profile of intelligences that interact, one with another, rather than a number of distinct intelligences. When we combine the ideas of potentials and profiles, we are reminded again that we can create robust learning activities that work with a number of intelligences, and there is no need to create eight or nine distinct learning centres.

Entry Points

It is helpful to think about the various intelligences as entry points to learning. Entry points describe what you might do when you are introducing new material to your class. They also describe what students might do when they are working with that material. If you present new material through multiple entry points, you give all students access to new learning through their various preferences. You also significantly increase the number of connections students can make to the learning, thereby increasing the likelihood that they will understand the new material.

Tell teachers that there are five entry points that are particularly useful, and possible, in classrooms. Give them each a copy of BLM 6.5, which is similar to the PowerPoint graphic. Ask them to take a minute to think of the subject area of their choice and reflect on which entry points they tend to use most frequently. Stress that the goal is to use as many entry points in introducing a new concept in a subject as possible. It is *not* about claiming that narrative is used in English class, logical/quantitative in Math class, and aesthetic in Art class. Ask teachers to put a checkmark on the entry points they are very comfortable using for most concepts, and a star on others.

Explain that you would like teachers to work with their grade or subject partners to explore a concept they are about to teach. (Note: If you have taught the Essential Understandings and Questions lesson in Chapter 7, refer to an essential understanding rather than a concept.) Ask them to move now to sit with their partners if they haven't already done so, to spend one minute deciding what concept/understanding they are going to explore, and to record that concept on their entry points blackline master.

Tell teachers that they are going to work on creating multiple entry points for the upcoming concept by using a differentiation structure called cubing. As the name suggests, cubing makes use of paper, plastic, or foam cubes with different questions or instructions written on each side. These cubes can be constructed, but you are going to use the least time-consuming option of using standard dice with corresponding instructions provided on PowerPoint slides. When using cubes with students, teachers can differentiate according to the level of the question, the strategies practised, or the entry point used.

Ask teachers to roll one die six times and come up with an activity for teaching their concept each time. If they roll one number more often than others, they need to come up with the corresponding number of activities for that entry point. Tell teachers that you will watch to see when most groups are finished and will bring everyone together for a conclusion to the workshop. Hand out dice and workshop assessment forms (BLM 3.2), advance the PowerPoint to the quotation on the next slide, and join teachers as they work.

Reconvene the group for the last five minutes of the workshop and invite comments and reflections on the activity. Ask teachers to look again at their entry points sheet and to circle the starred entry point that they intend to work on over the next while. Ask that they add this entry point to the bottom of their assessment form so that, even without their name, you will have useful information about entry points that many teachers on staff would like to develop. You can support them with resources, where possible. Thank participants for attending and for their enthusiastic involvement.

Sustain the Learning

Request that teachers include multiple entry points in their design of new units and lessons. Provide time for teachers to collaborate with grade or subject partners in this work if that is not already a common practice.

When you have taught the lesson on essential curriculum (Chapter 7, pages 92–96), choose a number of outcomes that develop across all grades and, in a half-day professional learning session, invite teachers to develop introductory lessons for each grade using multiple entry points. After teachers have tested and modified the lessons, keep them for future reference. If teachers are particularly keen, you may wish to videotape the lessons for self-assessment or for peer review.

Staff members with strengths in computer skills or data organization may be invited to develop a system or refine an existing one that allows current and future teachers to readily access and update positive learning-profile information about students.

Publish a copy of the entry points graphic in your family newsletter, along with the explanation that introducing new material to students in more than one form and allowing them to work with that material in more than one way enhances student understanding and their ability to transfer that understanding from one subject area or one concept to another. Include photographs and samples of student work to showcase the variety of entry points used in a single classroom or in classrooms across your school. Make sure you have discussed/shared the newsletter with staff before distribution so they do not feel that they have been pressured to teach in this way.

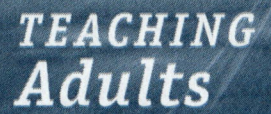

TEACHING Adults

40 minutes

STUDENT INTERESTS

Significance to student achievement	Learning is easiest when the information is personally relevant. In order to be relevant, new information has to link to something the student already knows. Therefore, if teachers know what their students are interested in, they have some established points of connection for new learning.
Common questions and issues	I give interest inventories at the beginning of the year, but then never know what to do with the results, other than try to provide books on the topics of a student's choice.
When would you use this lesson?	At any time during the year, but only if some teachers already make use of student interests in their planning and teaching and are willing to share/showcase their ideas.
Materials you need	• BLM 6.6 Stopping at a Lunchroom Table (1 per person or a single copy for someone to read aloud) • BLM 3.2 Workshop Assessment (1 per person, modified for this workshop)—optional
Suggested group set-up	Teacher choice

Build the Evidence Base

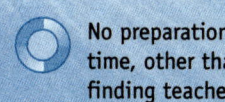

No preparation time, other than finding teachers

This workshop provides teachers with an opportunity to share and/or showcase the methods they use to determine students' interests and how they make use of those interests in their planning and teaching. There is no need for you to do anything in preparation for this workshop other than encourage teachers to share their knowledge and their teaching strengths.

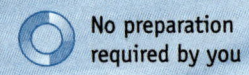 No preparation required by you

Teach the Session

The presenting teachers will develop this session as they wish. Offer them the short article "Stopping at a Lunchroom Table" by teacher and author Penny Kittle (2005), suggesting that it is available if they wish to share it with their colleagues before, during, or after the workshop. You might also offer the workshop assessment form (BLM 3.2), but stress that it is not necessary that they use this form or even do an assessment.

Sustain the Learning

Teaching others is one of the best ways to learn, so this session will have been a good professional learning situation for the presenting teachers. Talk with them about what they learned, acknowledge their work, and be on the lookout for other situations in which teachers will take the lead in developing and sharing ideas with their colleagues.

As a former teacher–librarian, I can confirm that, with the approach of any holiday, parents are looking for titles of books that will be of interest to their children. Why not start a regular newsletter column where your teacher–librarian, public librarian, interested teacher, or student can choose an interest (e.g., skateboarding) and provide their top five picks with cost, source, and a brief descriptor for each.

CHAPTER 7

Essential Understandings

CHAPTER AT A GLANCE

Section	Focus	Action/Time
Getting to Essential Understandings (p. 89)	What teachers need from administrators • A guaranteed and viable curriculum • Understanding of curriculum theory • Resource support	Read
Teaching Adults (p. 92)	Essential curriculum outcomes • Curricular approaches—activity, coverage, or results • Introducing *Understanding by Design* • Significance of essential curriculum • Sustain the learning—mapping curriculum across the grades	40 minutes plus, ideally, a half day for Sustain the Learning; no preparation required for the first session
Teaching Adults (p. 97)	Essential understandings and questions • Determining a unit's "big ideas" or essential understandings • Asking essential questions	40 minutes or more; no preparation required

MODEL FOCUS

Essential Understandings

Getting to Essential Understandings

The competing pressures to address curriculum guidelines, standardized, high-stakes tests, and the ever-growing demands of accountability for achievement can turn even the most dedicated and determined teacher into a "we have to keep moving; too bad if you can't keep up" curriculum coverage machine.

Teachers look to the school principal for permission to teach as they are supposed to—with the intention of uncovering the big ideas or essential understandings of their discipline, rather than covering and smothering those ideas with a focus on facts and drill.

"Uh-oh, teacher burnout!"

www.CartoonStock.com

The first of the Teaching Adults lessons in this chapter deals with the importance of a guaranteed and viable curriculum. This is a school-level factor for student achievement; in fact, it is *the* school-level factor that has the greatest impact on achievement (Marzano, 2003). Ensuring a guaranteed and viable curriculum requires that you work with staff to

- determine essential versus supplemental content
- make sure there is sufficient time to address the essential content
- monitor to ensure that the essential content is being taught

Because teachers will look to you for permission to focus on what matters, this first Teaching Adults session is one *you* should teach. Other instructional leaders can facilitate other sessions; this is the session where having the words come from the school principal really matters.

Once essential outcomes have been identified, they have to be taught in ways that promote understanding. To this end, the second lesson plan deals with the "big ideas" or essential understandings and essential questions of Grant Wiggins and Jay McTighe's *Understanding by Design* (2005; and see Learn More About on page 91). Understanding by Design (UbD) works very well with the constructivist, inquiry-based approach that provides multiple points of entry to learning for our diverse student population.

Inquiry-based learning is resource-rich learning, bringing us to the third point of needed administrator support. In an inquiry-based or constructivist classroom, students are examining significant concepts from a variety of perspectives and through a variety of entry points. A single textbook can never be adequate; a variety of textbooks is a little better, but by their very nature textbooks chunk big ideas into small, digestible bits, often to the point where it is difficult to recognize the idea and just as difficult to see

CALVIN AND HOBBES © 1993 Watterson. Dist. by UNIVERSAL PRESS SYNDICATE. Reprinted with permission. All rights reserved.

connections among the bits. For effective, differentiated instruction in support of essential understandings, students need access to a wide range of oral, print, and other media resources, including artifacts, DVDs or videos, the internet, photographs, works of art, and print materials of all forms. Public libraries, school board media libraries, and the loan departments of museums, galleries, and associations are all helpful, but they are not a substitute for the easy accessibility of well-stocked school and classroom libraries.

Most administrators are more than willing to invest in a wide range of resources, but are challenged when teachers request the purchase of varied resources *and* class sets of textbooks. If you are in this situation, you might want to resist purchasing new textbooks until after teachers have experienced both of the Teaching Adults lessons in this chapter as well as both Sustain the Learning activities. Then, strike a small textbook committee that will create a review form to assess texts against the material discussed in this chapter. Engagement in a systematic review process is a powerful form of professional learning in its own right, as well as placing ownership of resource purchases where it belongs—with the teachers who will use the resources.

If you are in a school division where texts are purchased centrally, consider striking a committee to examine how to make the best use of existing school resources. For example, perhaps texts can be grouped in small sets so that a number of different texts are still provided to each classroom.

Learn More About Understanding by Design

All of the *Understanding by Design* resources (video series, book, workbook, web exchange) are excellent. That said, if I only had money to purchase one of them, I would buy the workbook. It contains planning organizers, exercises, and process tools for workshops, and numerous examples from various subject areas and grade levels.

McTighe, J., & Wiggins, G. (2004). *Understanding by design professional development workbook*. Alexandria, Virginia: ASCD.

TEACHING Adults

ESSENTIAL CURRICULUM OUTCOMES

 40 minutes

Significance to student achievement	Students cannot achieve essential outcomes that have not been taught. Teachers can be very good at differentiating instruction, but if they are differentiating meaningless or irrelevant work, their efforts will not result in achievement of meaningful, important outcomes.
Common questions and issues	• When the curriculum is mandated, what choice do I have but to give every outcome equal weight and equal time? • My students, and their parents, just love my unit on _____. It is a rite of passage, a tradition. Don't ask me to give it up just because it doesn't address the outcomes!
When would you use this lesson?	This session is applicable to your entire staff at any point during the school year; however, given the central role of curriculum in a school, you may want to teach this session early in the year. This session will be particularly important to offer if you are new to the school because teachers will want to know your position on the issue of curriculum coverage.
Materials you need	• Essential Curriculum PowerPoint presentation and equipment to show it • Sheet of flipchart paper and marker or whiteboard and marker • BLM 3.2 Workshop Assessment (1 per person, modified for this workshop) • Work Kit (1 per group)
Suggested group set-up	Teacher choice

92 Chapter 7

Build the Evidence Base

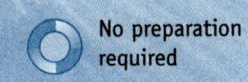 No preparation required

You will not need to take deliberate steps to build an evidence base to either support the need for this workshop or to recognize the difference in staff if their actions change after the workshop is completed. Since curriculum and its "coverage" are central teacher responsibilities, this workshop is undoubtedly a good idea. It becomes an essential good idea if in your school you see

- holiday curriculum—the Thanksgiving unit followed by Remembrance Day, followed by Christmas
- an activity-driven curriculum—a busy, perhaps engaging, classroom but without clearly identified goals for all of the activity

and/or if you hear teachers

- complaining that the previous teacher didn't adequately prepare students for this year
- expressing the need to dash through the curriculum regardless of student understanding because "there's just so much to cover"

Teach the Session

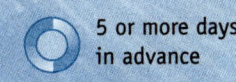 5 or more days in advance

Please refer to Chapter 7, Session 1 PowerPoint file.

Have this first slide projected, and greet people as they arrive.

Comment to staff that there are reasons we still plan units based on engaging activities or huge events. To set a positive tone for the remainder of the workshop, begin by telling one of your own stories, communicating both your fond memory of the unit and, if felt, your acknowledgment that the learning may have been sparse.

Then encourage teachers to share memories of the unit plan they may have written in teacher's college that gave Grade 3 students a four-week crash course in the complete works of Shakespeare, or the time in Grade 5 when they dressed as a medieval serf and ate with their hands. Because this activity builds a warm feeling of "we have all been there," have the stories shared with the whole group. If the group is large, have each person share with a partner, followed by a few people who would like to share their memories with the entire group.

Before the storytelling ends, ensure teachers are starting to question the learning that was supposed to take place. If necessary, gently probe for the academic purpose of the unit, whether or not the teacher thought it was achieved, and how they might know. You may want to encourage teachers to create a three-column chart they can complete during the storytelling; headings are Purpose, Achievements, and Indicators of Achievement.

Discuss the concept (recording on chart paper or whiteboard) that there are three basic approaches to planning curriculum—the activity approach, the coverage approach, and the results approach. Invite other suggestions.

Explain that the *Understanding by Design* concept by Grant Wiggins and Jay McTighe is about planning from results. The focus, then, is on the learner and what she or he needs to understand, know, and be able to do, before thought is given to what the teacher will do. Reinforce that this approach is backwards to activity or coverage approaches, both of which begin with an emphasis on what teachers will do. Focusing on the learner will lead to better teaching.

Emphasize the links among the three stages of backward design, and that the sheep is a mnemonic device to remind us that unit planning—backwards or forwards—is not a lockstep, sequential process. It is more like the untangling of a ball of wool with leads to follow, and the need to work back and forth along the strand in order to smooth out the kinks.

Advise teachers that this model looks simple but, because of our experiences, we have built-in expectations about the way a unit should be structured. These expectations can make it difficult to think about unit planning in a new way. Tell staff that their collaboration and support of one another will make it an enjoyable experience for all. Explain that today, and for the next while, they will be working with the first piece of the *Understanding by Design* template, namely the focus on desired results.

Use this slide to introduce the significance of essential curriculum. Talk about the fact that all outcomes in a curriculum guide do not deserve equal attention. Explain that the authors of *Understanding by Design* labelled this the Goldilocks problem to remind us that there are often a number of curriculum outcomes that are too small, too insignificant, or too limited to deserve serious attention. Reassure anxious teachers that those expectations can be addressed under broader headings, and that the process of establishing essential understandings will result in those broad headings.

Stress that just as outcomes can be too small, they can also be too large. Say that outcomes that are too large are unmanageable in the time teachers have available to teach, and that they are so vague they end up being interpreted in many different ways, with the result that the concept of "essential" is lost.

Discuss how the establishment of essential goals involves the entire staff working together to map the progression of curriculum outcomes across the grades, identifying what is truly important for both the next grade's work and for key points of standardized assessment. Refer back to the paper or whiteboard where you noted the three approaches to curriculum, and underline "results." Comment that activity is exciting and memorable, and there is still plenty of room for great activities *if* they emerge from a focus on results. Note that no one mentioned a fond memory of a worksheet or textbook page they completed, yet that, plus direct instruction, is the work we are often forced into if we focus on equal coverage of every expectation.

Explain the next step in this work (see Sustain the Learning, below) and thank teachers for attending and sharing their experiences. Ask teachers to complete the Workshop Assessment before they leave (BLM 3.2).

Sustain the Learning

A logical next step for the focus on essential curriculum is to devote a minimum of a half day to having staff map the progression of essential curriculum outcomes across the grades, identifying what is important for the next grade's work and for any standardized assessments. This is a useful exercise even if your province or district has already done a good job of identifying and sequencing essential outcomes. We tend to focus only on the piece of curriculum that is our responsibility and to ignore the rest. The review of all grades makes it easier to spot the essential understandings of a discipline and the way they build over a student's years in school, as well as the importance of each teacher's role in working with those understandings.

To conduct a comprehensive curriculum review, include all teachers, not only those in your school, but perhaps also those in the next grade that your students attend when they leave your school. Put teachers in subject or cross-grade groupings, and give each teacher packages of green, yellow, and red dots so they can quickly and easily mark each outcome in a curriculum guide. Through discussion, teachers should arrive at consensus and mark outcomes as essential (green), important (yellow), and nice to know but not critical (red). A range of the amount of time necessary to teach each green outcome should be given and totals calculated to ensure that there is sufficient time in the instructional day and year to teach essential curriculum and yet still allow some time for important topics, serendipitous events, or student interests. If you work in a district where all outcomes must be explicitly addressed, stress that while the primary focus of a particular unit is on essential outcomes, the outcomes identified by red dots will be included through skilful planning.

Once essential curriculum goals are established, ask teachers to highlight these essentials in their personal copies of the curriculum guides and to again use the dots, this time putting green dots on each essential outcome they teach effectively, yellow on those that need more emphasis, and red on those outcomes that are not addressed. As teachers become more confident teaching essential outcomes, they can change yellow and red dots to green (Chapman and King, 2005). Note that if your curriculum guides have already identified essentials, there is no need for teachers to recreate this process. Stress that the dot activity is intended to focus on what the teacher teaches from the curriculum, rather than what the curriculum says they should teach.

Ask various groups of teachers to take a single essential outcome, trace its development through the grades, and represent it in a meaningful graphic organizer. Display these representations at parent–teacher curriculum events and/or include them in issues of your newsletter.

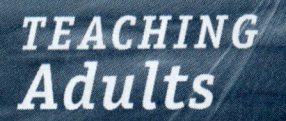
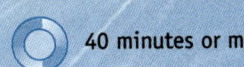

Essential Understandings and Questions

Significance to student achievement	Phrasing curriculum outcomes in terms of essential understandings supports students in making connections and transfers of understanding across subject and grade levels. Phrasing understandings in the form of essential questions helps to increase the relevancy of the learning for students and encourages the focus on inquiry that is necessary for deep understanding.
Common questions and issues	• What is the difference between essential curriculum outcomes and essential understandings? • What makes a question "essential"?
When would you use this lesson?	Teach this session as a follow-up to the session on essential curriculum (see page 92) and a completion of the "Desired Results" segment of the Understanding by Design approach.
Materials you need	• *Understanding by Design* PowerPoint presentation and necessary equipment • Work Kit (1 per group) • 3 signs to post on wall—Know/Understand That/Be Able To • BLM 3.2 Workshop Assessment (1 per person, modified for this workshop)
Suggested group set-up	Subject or grade-level partners

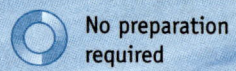

Build the Evidence Base

Since curriculum and its "coverage" is one of a teacher's central responsibilities, this workshop is automatically relevant. It becomes essential if, in your school, you see long-range plans with unit headings that are lists of expectations or are topics rather than concepts, or if you hear a student saying "I don't know" when you ask why they are engaged in a particular activity.

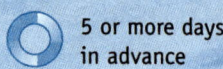

Teach the Session

Please refer to Chapter 7, Session 2 PowerPoint file.

Welcome participants. Drawing their attention to the *Success for Every Student* model, note that today's workshop deals with essential understandings, a condition of effectiveness in teaching, and a precondition of effective differentiated instruction. Stress that essential understandings emerge from curriculum expectations or outcomes and are *not* differentiated. Differentiation is in *how* students learn, not in *what* they learn.

If teachers have already attended the session on essential curriculum, they will be familiar with this slide of Wiggins and McTighe's stages of backward design. Show it again to establish context for today's session. Explain that once again you will be focusing only on the first bubble of "Identify Results."

Indicate that results are identified in terms of what a student will understand, know, and be able to do. Point out the significance of the word "that" as in "will understand that." Explain that the use of this word helps us to focus our attention on understanding rather than knowledge. Give an example such as "Students will understand that metaphors are a poetic way of noting similarities and differences between two objects or ideas" as opposed to "Students will understand metaphors." The first statement makes the expectation clear and can be satisfied only by a demonstration of understanding; the second is less clear and can be satisfied by a demonstration of knowledge, such as the student being able to select metaphors from a list.

Explain that if we leave desired results at the level of essential outcomes, the language isn't very student-friendly and, more importantly, it is too easy to lose our focus on understanding. Say that to focus on understanding rather than just factual knowledge, we need to uncover the "big ideas" or essential understandings of our curriculum outcomes.

Together, discuss how big ideas are the umbrella understandings that are at the core of a discipline. They are the source of continuous exploration and learning, even for experts in that discipline. Big ideas stimulate thought, alternative points of view, and passionate discussion. Give teachers the tip that big ideas can often be found by looking at the recurring nouns and adjectives in their curriculum documents.

Project this slide and ask teachers to work in their groups to generate fictitious curriculum outcomes, both essential and trivial, that would work with this Ziggy cartoon. The outcomes should be written in the form of "The student will understand that . . . ," "The student will know . . . ," and "The student will be able to . . . ." Once written, have teachers post outcomes on the wall and review those posted by others. Ask that multiple expressions of the same outcome not be posted.

Review the postings on the wall and help teachers understand that essential content understandings will appear under the heading "The student will understand that . . . " while essential skills will appear under the heading "The student will be able to . . . ."

Explain that in Wiggins and McTighe's work, essential skills are referred to as core tasks and are focused on the techniques, procedures, and skills that are essential to competence in a discipline. Note that teachers can find core task ideas by looking at the verbs that recur in their curriculum documents. Discuss how core tasks are best demonstrated by providing students with authentic assessments in which they will use the skills and procedures that are essential to the discipline. Invite teachers to speak to the essential math and science skills necessary to Ziggy's discussion of validity.

Explain that in order to encourage students to inquire and develop understanding, rather than just look something up and remember facts, the big ideas need to be framed in the form of questions. Discuss how really great essential questions go to the heart of the discipline. Essential questions never have easy answers that a student can simply look up in a book. Further, they are framed in student-friendly language or, better still, are generated by teachers and students working together.

Ask teachers to come to a group decision about whether or not Ziggy's query about validation is an essential question. They should report their decision and rationale to the whole group.

Essential Understandings

Explain the next step in this work (see Sustain the Learning), and thank teachers for attending and sharing their experiences. Ask teachers to complete the Workshop Assessment before they leave (BLM 3.2).

Sustain the Learning

Provide teachers with an opportunity to work with the concepts of essential understandings (including core tasks) and essential questions soon after they have completed the workshop. It is best if this is structured planning time of a half day or more. Teachers could be asked to

- experiment with these ideas in an upcoming unit and invite you or a colleague to visit during an inquiry or the development of essential questions

- plan an upcoming unit, preferably in collaboration with others, according to essential understandings and essential questions, then teach the unit and evaluate its impact on students

- review an existing unit of their own or one they have downloaded from the internet, revising it so that outcome language is in the form of "know, understand that, and able to do," and, if it is a unit they intend to use, writing a core demonstration task for a summative assessment and essential questions that promote inquiry

Support teachers with a book study of Wiggins and McTighe's *Understanding by Design* (2005) or their *Understanding by Design Professional Development Workbook* (2004).

Show your support of teaching that is centred around inquiry, problem-solving, and critical thinking by spending time in those classrooms, by expressing your interest in the work, and by publicly praising teachers for the great learning that you are seeing.

CHAPTER 8
Assessment for Learning (Pre-Assessments)

CHAPTER AT A GLANCE

Section	Focus	Action/Time
Pre-Assessing Knowledge and Attitude (p. 101)	The significance of pre-assessments to differentiated instruction	Read
Process (p. 103)	Using self-reports and quick writes to pre-assess teacher knowledge and attitude	Read
Teaching Adults (p. 108)	Understanding the value of pre-assessing students Identifying criteria of a good pre-assessment Modelling the use of pre-assessments to group for learning Differentiation structure—grouping for learning	30 minutes for session plus 30 minutes for preparation, including gathering evidence

MODEL FOCUS

Evidence Base
Knowledge of Students

Pre-Assessing Knowledge and Attitude

Pre-assessments, or diagnostic assessments, provide valuable information about each individual's background experience, knowledge base, misconceptions, level of skill, and/or attitude relative to a particular concept or upcoming unit of study. When this information is combined with knowledge of the individual's learning preferences and interests, the teacher is better able to group students appropriately for learning and to determine the kinds of activities that will best engage and support each learner.

Pre-assessing an individual's knowledge, skill, or attitude is a cornerstone activity of a differentiating teacher and, to an only slightly lesser extent, of a differentiating administrator. "Only slightly lesser" acknowledges that adult learners come to most situations with extensive background knowledge and experience, an awareness of their own learning preferences and strengths, and a drive to seek relevance in their learning. They will make many learning connections on their own. However, teachers, like any other learners, appreciate instructors who "walk the talk." If you are going to encourage teachers to differentiate instruction and be responsive to the needs of individual learners, you want to show them that pre-assessments are easy to do and that the information gleaned from the pre-assessments will lead to greater effectiveness and efficiency for them when planning and delivering lessons, just as understanding of your teachers' knowledge, attitudes, and skills will help to guide you.

Pre-assessments allow you to be both more effective and more efficient in your instruction because you don't waste time and energy working on material learners have already mastered or are not yet ready to master. However, pre-assessments are only useful when you are clear about and assessing for the concepts learners need to understand (essential understandings) and the skills they need to be able to demonstrate after your teaching.

Once learning goals are clearly established, refer to BLM 8.3 for tips on writing a useful pre-assessment. When considering adult learners, pay particular attention to surfacing misconceptions about aspects of teaching and learning. Misconceptions will colour perceptions and affect learning. They need to be identified and addressed through the provision of learning experiences that lead to a new perspective.

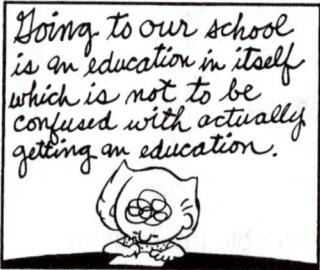

Peanuts: © United Feature Syndicate, Inc.

PROCESS

Pre-Assessing Teacher Knowledge Using Self-Reports and Quick Writes

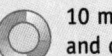
10 minutes to photocopy and distribute

What Are They?

Classroom walk-throughs (Chapter 1, page 17), one-legged interviews (Chapter 3, page 41), and reflective conversations (Chapter 5, page 69) are three processes that provide rich, detailed pre-assessment data. However, several of the pre-assessment tools that teachers use with students work equally well in pre-assessing teacher attitudes and knowledge. Two of the simpler ones are self-reports and quick writes.

A self-report, as the name suggests, invites participants to make their own assessments, usually of their attitude toward a topic or their confidence in engaging in a particular activity. Self-reports include a number of paired statements (one positive, one negative, separated in the assessment) about each variable to be explored. Participants rank their responses from Strongly Agree to Strongly Disagree or from Very Confident to Not Confident. If a self-report is perceived by the participants to be completely anonymous, teachers will get valid group summaries of attitude, which they can use in their planning. Anonymous self-reports are not useful for individual assessments of attitude, however; because attitude is demonstrated through behaviour, teachers need to observe students to assess individual attitudes.

Quick writes provide learners with limited periods of time, often five minutes or less, to write everything they know about a topic. There are various ways to encourage students to provide lots of information in quick writes. For example, a pair of contrasting prompts can be given and students asked to write or discuss their responses to each in turn. Here are some examples:

- I can explain/I can't explain
- I know/I don't know
- I remember/I forget
- I like/I dislike
- I'm looking forward to/I'm not looking forward to

- I am interested in/I am not interested in
- I'm good at/I'm not good at
- I believe/I don't believe

For the purpose of the Teaching Adults session in this chapter, you will pre-assess teachers' knowledge and attitudes toward pre-assessing students. To do so, you can use a modified version of a combined self-report and quick write, such as the one provided in BLM 8.1. It asks participants to choose one of three simple statements that will allow you to sort participants into three groups. This is followed by a quick write using the prompts "I know/I don't know" to give you more information about the needs of the individuals within each of the three groups. Note that you will want to be sensitive to your staff's comfort with the prompts you use. If people are uncomfortable acknowledging what they don't know, change the prompts to one of the other prompt pairings suggested above. Do try to make sure you use a contrasting pair of prompts rather than a single one; contrasting prompts encourage a wider range of responses.

How Do You Do Them?

1. Decide what you would like teachers to know, understand, and be able to do by the end of a workshop. Focus on larger concepts and skills rather than discrete facts. (See Chapter 7.)

2. Construct a pre-assessment that will allow you to measure teachers' current levels of understanding or skill, or their attitude toward a topic. (See BLM 8.1.) Your pre-assessment has to have only enough detail to allow you to mentally divide your staff into three or four groups, and to be responsive to the particular needs of each group.

3. Administer the pre-assessments and collect the results.

4. Use the results of the pre-assessments to group individuals for learning. Depending on what you asked on the pre-assessment, groups may be based on content knowledge, skill development, preferred entry points for learning, an appropriate LOPI (Levels of Program Implementation) chart, or a model of individual change such as the Concerns-Based Adoption Model. (See Chapter 3.) Groupings may be obvious (individuals asked to sit together) or subtle (you keep individuals' starting points in mind as you teach).

5. Provide differentiated instruction or support to the groups you have established.

When Do You Do Them?

Administer pre-assessments far enough in advance of a professional learning opportunity that the facilitator, whether you or someone else, has time to use the results in the planning.

Why Do Them?

- When you know what participants already understand, teaching can be more appropriately targeted to encourage and support new learning.
- Pre-assessment data allows you to use differentiated structures such as grouping learners for specific, short-term tasks that address their needs and/or preferences.
- Pre-assessments are an example of data that are easy to collect and useful in informing instruction. You model both features for teachers through your own use of pre-assessments.
- Self-reports and quick writes are fast pre-assessments that teachers may not be familiar with but would find easy to use.

Who Does Them?

The person responsible for planning and facilitating the professional learning workshop creates the pre-assessment. Participants who attend the workshop need to complete the pre-assessment, particularly if the results are going to be used to differentiate instruction.

Q & A: Pre-Assessments

Q. The pre-assessments you suggest require teachers to complete something in writing and hand it in. Some of my teachers aren't great at the "complete and hand in" request. How do I improve the rate of return?

A. If the lack of compliance is forgetfulness or procrastination, not resistance, there are several things you can do:
- Make the pre-assessment short and simple. Ideally, it should consist of half a page and require five minutes or less to complete.

- Use paper that stands out from the other paperwork your teachers have to deal with by choosing a colour or design that you don't normally use or that you use only to indicate to your teachers that you are requesting their response.
- Clearly state that the purpose of the pre-assessment is to personalize and improve the quality of an upcoming workshop.
- Take advantage of small windows of time. For example, ask division chair people to have everyone complete the pre-assessment during the first five minutes of another meeting.
- Offer small rewards and have some fun with it! In my first year of teaching, an administrator walked into my classroom, handed me a candy, and said, "You've heard of the carrot and the stick? Here's the carrot." I laughed, and handed in the outstanding form.

Q. Some of my teachers are unwilling to complete any extra paperwork. Are pre-assessments worth the battle? If so, how do I get around the resistors?

A. If your explanation that the pre-assessment is intended to improve the quality of the workshop doesn't help (and sometimes it doesn't), here are a few options to try:

- Complete the pre-assessment through a brief, informal conversation so there is no requirement for paperwork.
- Find out the source of the resistance and take steps to counteract it. For example, if the issue is unwillingness to complete paperwork outside of teaching time, schedule the five minutes the pre-assessment will take during regular school hours—perhaps at the start or end of another meeting, or at the end of the previous workshop.
- Decide that it is not worth fighting this particular battle with this particular individual. If you choose this route, assign the teacher to a group based on your classroom observations or your best guess of needs and strengths. Continue to invite the teacher to participate in any pre-assessments you give in the future.

Q. I'm surprised that you recommend grouping people for learning. Aren't ability groups a bad idea?

A. Ability groups are a bad idea because they are long-term, inflexible, based on a broad, generic assessment of overall ability, and often focus on weaknesses rather than strengths. Grouping for learning, on the other hand, is a key practice of a differentiating teacher. Groups are short-term, flexible, and based on clearly identified and specific criteria.

Q. In order to group my teachers (even when I'm just grouping them mentally according to how I can support them), the pre-assessments can't be anonymous. They might see that as pretty risky. How do I ensure a feeling of safety for all participants?

A. This is the same dilemma faced by teachers in a classroom, particularly in a classroom of young adolescents (grades 6–8) where difference from peers is often considered unacceptable. Draw teachers' attention to the similarities with their classroom experience and ask them how they build a classroom learning community based on recognition and appreciation of individuals' different starting points. (See Chapter 5 for a discussion of classroom and adult learning communities, and Chapter 6 for information about recognizing and appreciating strengths.)

Q. I require my teachers to administer standardized tests at the beginning of the year in order to determine what students know and can do in reading, writing, and mathematics. Is there really a need for further diagnostics?

A. Standardized tests consist of a common set of items administered to all students under uniform conditions. As long as those conditions are met, you can make valid comparisons between groups of students and among individual students. Standardized tests can be reassuring because of their high degree of reliability (scoring stays consistent across all students) and validity (the test measures what it purports to measure). They are useful in order to determine district level professional learning needs, and they can be helpful at the classroom level to determine reading or math skills. The problem with standardized tests is they are often standardized on large populations of students from a number of provinces or states, meaning that the questions cannot be specific to your curriculum. They include relatively few items and so provide only a general level of achievement in a broad academic area. If you intend to use standardized tests at the beginning of a year, help your teachers to see their value as general diagnostic instruments, rather than as replacements for pre-assessments conducted prior to various units of study.

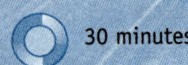

Using Pre-Assessments to Group for Learning

TEACHING Adults — 30 minutes

Significance to student achievement	Pre-assessments allow teachers to be both more effective and more efficient in their instruction by targeting specific learning needs of individuals, while grouping those learners so the teacher is not creating 30 individualized programs.
Common questions and issues	• What is the value of pre-assessing student knowledge, skills, or attitude? • What are the criteria of a useful pre-assessment? • How are pre-assessments used in a differentiated classroom?
When would you use this lesson?	This session is applicable to your entire staff at any point during the school year.

Materials you need	• BLM 8.1 Two Simple Pre-Assessment Tools: Self-Report and Quick Write (1 per person in advance of session)
	• Work Kit (1 per group)
	• Three goals of the session recorded on chart paper (optional)
	• BLM 8.2 Grouping Learners for Pre-Assessment Workshop (1 per facilitator)
	• BLM 8.3 Criteria of a Good and Useful Pre-Assessment (1 per person)
	• Task cards (see BLM 8.4 Group Task Cards; 1 card per group). Distribute the cards as follows:
	  - the group that doesn't pre-assess gets Task Card 1
	  - the group that pre-assesses occasionally gets Task Card 2
	  - the group that pre-assesses routinely gets Task Card 3
	• chart paper (2–3 sheets for Group 1)
	• lined paper (half a dozen sheets for groups 2 and 3)
	• extra pre-assessments (see step 5 of Build the Evidence Base)—optional
	• BLM 3.2 Workshop Assessment (1 per person, modified for this workshop)

| **Suggested group set-up** | Three groups, as determined by your work in Build the Evidence Base. Choose three colours or designs of stickers—one for each group. Put a sticker on each teacher's pre-assessment to indicate their group, and a matching identifier at tables in the workshop room. Return pre-assessments to teachers as they enter the workshop so they know where to sit. |

Build the Evidence Base

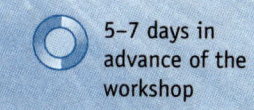

5–7 days in advance of the workshop

1. Copy BLM 8.1 and distribute to teachers, indicating a requested date for return. Alternatively, conduct brief, informal conversations with individual teachers, using the questions on BLM 8.1. Encourage them to administer pre-assessments several weeks in advance of a unit so they have time to use the data as they plan their lessons. Although you won't need much time to plan a single 30-minute workshop, you do need sufficient time to chase missing responses so you can be ready with learning groups prior to the session. If you wish, there is no harm in administering pre-assessments weeks in advance. You may even want to have teachers complete the forms at the end of a prior Teaching Adults workshop.

2. Group teachers according to their responses on the self-report section of your pre-assessment. Record the groupings on BLM 8.2.

3. Use BLM 8.2 to also record your teachers' responses to the quick write prompts. Here is an example of a completed grouping form:

Group	Who is in group?	What do they know?	What don't they know?
Don't pre-assess	Jordan	Pre-assessment a good idea, but too busy	What to do with them? Supposed to mark?
Pre-assess occasionally	Travis, Barb, Sakiko, Ian, Ahmed	How to use them in math—math textbook provides good examples (Travis, Barb, Ahmed)	Other pre-tests besides the ones in math textbook (Travis, Barb, Ahmed) How to mark? How to use in planning?

Assessment for Learning (Pre-Assessments)

Group	Who is in group?	What do they know?	What don't they know?
Pre-assess routinely	Cathy, Donovan, Sunita, Devon, Mary, Chris, Kim, Dave	Useful for determining starting points Are reminded of students' interests so can incorporate those interests into unit	Can they determine how much a student has learned during a unit? Is there a best kind of pre-assessment?

4. Use the completed BLM 8.2 to clarify the needs of your teachers as you plan your session. For example, as facilitator of the groups shown in the sample above, you might decide that the following actions are necessary:

- Although Jordan is the only teacher who admitted to not using pre-assessments at all, Travis, Barb, and Ahmed don't have any more experience with them than Jordan. Their use of pre-assessments consists only of the pre-assessments available in their math textbooks, and they don't use them for planning. Therefore Jordan, Travis, Barb, and Ahmed could be appropriately grouped together, regardless of the differences in their self-reports.

- Several teachers expressed a belief that pre-assessments should be marked. This reveals a misconception about the purpose of pre-assessments. Left unchecked, this will seriously diminish both the power of pre-assessments for informing instruction and the validity of a student's final grade. You decide to either modify your activity so that the teachers discover for themselves that pre-assessments should not be marked, or to explicitly discuss this misconception in your opening remarks.

- As Kim and Sunita have a solid understanding of how to use pre-assessments in planning, you talk to them in advance and ask if you may call on them for examples during the workshop or to work one-on-one with interested colleagues after the workshop.

Your analysis of your pre-assessment data may show that all of your teachers have about the same experience with pre-assessments, making distinct groups impractical. In that case, simply ignore the grouping suggestions made in Teach the Session and have everyone doing the same activity. Differentiated instruction is unnecessary when everyone is learning from a similar starting point.

5. Ask teachers to bring at least one example, preferably more, of pre-assessments they have seen or used—whether their own or ones photocopied from textbooks—to the workshop. Ask a few teachers to bring extra copies in case others arrive without examples.

Teach the Session

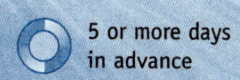
5 or more days in advance

Greet participants, give them their completed pre-assessment form, and invite them to sit in the group that matches their sticker colour.

Thank everyone for attending and for taking the time to complete the pre-assessment. Review the three goals of the session, which are to

- understand the value of pre-assessing students
- identify criteria of a good pre-assessment and use it to assess existing pre-assessments and/or create new ones
- model the use of pre-assessments to group for learning

Note that the groupings you have created address the third goal.

Explain the difference between ability groups and short-term, flexible groups based on common experience, understanding, interest, or need. (See Q & A: Pre-Assessments, pages 105–107, for more information.) Ask participants to reflect for a moment individually and then talk with their group members about what conditions need to be in place in a classroom or school for students (or teachers) to feel comfortable working in pre-arranged groups.

If you have already held the Teaching Adults session on Teacher Presence with the same group of teachers, refer back to the ideas discussed in that session (See Chapter 5, pages 66–68). If you haven't, be sure to discuss the importance of creating a safe and supportive environment in which all students feel recognized and accepted. The goal is to create classrooms where students are comfortable working in groups that are sometimes formed in response to interest, sometimes by shared experiences or level of understanding, and sometimes according to strengths.

Note: If teachers don't feel safe, you will see it in their response to being grouped for this session. Be prepared to spend time talking about the development of an effective learning community at both adult and student levels. The discussion may derail your intended focus on pre-assessments, but you can use that to your advantage, explaining that a safe and supportive environment is necessary before academic achievement can be realized. If teachers believe that pre-assessments should be counted toward report card grades, this is a good time to talk about why that is not the case.

Advise teachers that the next 10–15 minutes will be devoted to working in their small groups with the pre-assessments they have brought. Explain that groups in a differentiated classroom are all working toward the same goals—point to your list of goals—but that each group begins from a different starting point and therefore requires different activities, which may vary significantly or slightly. Mention to teachers that at the end of their work session you will invite them to share their activity, and whether or not it was helpful to them as a learner, with the whole group.

Distribute individual copies of BLM 8.3 (Criteria of a Good and Useful Pre-Assessment), and group copies of the appropriate task cards from BLM 8.4. Circulate and offer support as groups do their work.

Debrief with the whole group by having each small group share their activity and whether or not it promoted their learning. Point out the subtle differences between activities, again stressing that differentiated instruction helps people "start where they are" and progress from that point. Acknowledge that the pre-assessment you asked teachers to complete does not meet all of the criteria of a "good and useful pre-assessment," yet it gave you sufficient information so you could easily create the various group activities.

Encourage teachers to experiment with pre-assessments for an upcoming unit, and thank them for their involvement in this session. Ask that they complete the Workshop Assessment form (BLM 3.2) before they leave.

Sustain the Learning

Request that teachers share pre-assessments with you when you visit their classrooms, and with their colleagues at grade, divisional, or whole-staff meetings. In all situations, teachers should be asked what they learned about their students from the pre-assessment and how this data has informed their teaching.

In your family newsletter, write to parents about the importance of background knowledge and the ways in which they can extend and enrich the background knowledge of students of all ages. You might want to include the following, personalized with details relevant to your school community:

> When your child is learning something new, such as double-digit multiplication in Mr. Lee's Grade 3 class, or how bodies were mummified in Mrs. Airdrie's unit on Ancient Egypt, your child's teacher first checks to see what your child already knows about the topic. These pre-assessments, or diagnostic assessments, aren't for marks on the report

card. Your child's teacher uses them to plan for instruction because effective instruction is based on starting at your child's current level of understanding and building from there.

Educational researchers have found that what students already know about a topic makes a significant difference to their success in learning new information. Researchers refer to this prior knowledge as "background knowledge." When the background knowledge is about things that are important in school, a child's achievement in school increases.

It is never too late to enhance your child's background knowledge. Here are some ways:

→ *Read! Reading is a form of virtual experience and a great way to build vocabulary. Students should read what they are interested in, or listen to you reading it to them. Gradually work at building and extending those interests. Mrs. Scott, our librarian, can help you with suggestions, as can the wonderful staff at the _____ Public Library.*

→ *Take field trips to museums, art galleries, science centres, the farm down the road . . . . New experiences are the most direct and straightforward way to increase a child's background knowledge, and they don't have to be expensive.*

→ *Talk with your child, using a wide variety of words in context. There is good evidence to suggest that the broader a child's vocabulary, the more connections established in the brain and therefore the more extensive the background knowledge that can be accessed. For example, a student who can name kinds of trees has more connection points than one who knows that there are two types of trees—coniferous (cone-bearing) and deciduous (sheds leaves), and that student has more connection points than a student who simply knows they are all trees.*

→ *Watch television or play computer games. Before your children get too excited about this suggestion, please note that television programs or computer games intended for entertainment will do nothing to enhance background knowledge. For the program or game to be useful, it has to be "educational," meaning that the content is directly related to something your child is or will be studying in school. Children benefit from your involvement in the program or game.*

Learn More About the Significance of Background Knowledge

If you are in a community where parents do not view school knowledge as significant or where their lives allow little leisure for extending students' background knowledge, there are a number of steps you can take at school to level the playing field between those students who have had experiences and those who have not. Robert Marzano's work on enriching students' academic vocabulary is particularly interesting.

For research information and details on how to set up a school-wide vocabulary program, see Marzano, R. (2004). *Building background knowledge for academic achievement.* Alexandria, Virginia: ASCD.

For teacher support material, including how to teach new terms and review games and activities, see Marzano, R., & Pickering, D. (2005). *Building academic vocabulary* (teacher's manual). Alexandria, Virginia: ASCD.

CHAPTER 9

Powerful Instructional Strategies

CHAPTER AT A GLANCE

Section	Focus	Action/Time
Instructional Strategies (p. 115)	Marzano's nine categories of instructional strategies	Read
Process (p. 118)	Classroom observation—what to watch for in a strategy lesson	20–40 minutes per teacher; timing dependent on purpose
Teaching Adults (p. 121)	Introduction to the top nine strategies	10-minute session to be combined with Sustain the Learning of the same lesson or with Similarities and Differences; 5 minutes of preparation
Teaching Adults (p. 124)	Similarities and differences • Comparison • Classification • Metaphor • Analogy Differentiation structure—learning centres	40 minutes, plus 40 minutes of preparation

MODEL FOCUS

Powerful Instructional Strategies

Instructional Strategies

Talk of instructional strategies began in earnest approximately 25 years ago when researchers identified the reading strategies that good readers use to understand what they read. From there, it was a very small step to suggesting that struggling readers be let in on the secrets by being taught explicitly what good readers already know how to do.

In his review of the last 35 years of educational research, Robert Marzano (2003) applied the statistical process of meta-analysis to all of the various instructional strategies that were discussed in that research. He determined that there are nine categories of instructional strategies that, when properly taught, will have a significant, demonstrable, and measurable impact on the achievement of all students, in all subjects, at all grade levels. We don't know yet if some strategies are more effective with some students than others or if some are more appropriate to some grades than others, but we do know that these nine categories of strategies make a significant difference to student achievement. The following table lists the nine categories.

Categories of Instructional Strategies That Affect Student Achievement

Category	Percentile Gain
Identifying similarities and differences	45
Summarizing and note-taking	34
Reinforcing effort and providing recognition	29
Homework and practice	29
Nonlinguistic representations	27
Cooperative learning	27
Setting objectives and providing feedback	23
Generating and testing hypotheses	23
Questions, cues, and advance organizers	22

Source: Adapted from Marzano, Pickering and Pollock 2001:7

Every time I introduce Marzano's strategies to a group of teachers, the response is an audible collective sigh of relief and a sharp increase in attention. They appreciate knowing that certain strategies are worth their time. They enjoy exploring a strategy in detail, learning the steps involved in explicitly teaching it (if it is one that is directly taught to students), and then applying their subject knowledge and knowledge of their students to these steps in order to make them their own. Best of all, for our purposes in this guide, structures that support differentiated instruction are easy to implement in connection with powerful instructional strategies.

Teachers leave a strategy session with the tools to be simultaneously more effective with their entire class *and* more responsive to individuals.

Copyright Grantland Enterprises; www.grantland.net.

The Teaching Adults session in this chapter is concerned with the first of the nine categories of strategies, and includes an introductory piece that explains Marzano's research and provides his listing of all nine categories. The inclusion of details for only one strategy in this book is a deliberate reminder that school administrators need to be instructional leaders, but are not alone in that responsibility. If teachers express an interest in one of the eight other strategies, loan them your copies of Marzano's books (see Learn More About, below), provide a bit of preparation time if you can, and invite them to create a workshop for their peers, engage in action research about the strategy, lead a book club, or participate in any number of the other professional learning actions listed on page 49 of Chapter 4.

Learn More About Powerful Instructional Strategies

A copy of this first book belongs on every administrator's bookshelf, and in the hands of teachers who would like to understand each strategy and the most effective ways to teach them.

Marzano, R., Pickering, D., & Pollock, J. (2001). *Classroom instruction that works: Research-based strategies for increasing student achievement.* Alexandria, Virginia: ASCD.

The handbook contains some useful blackline masters and reflection prompts, along with information about each strategy.

Marzano, R., Norford, J., Paynter, D., Pickering, D., & Gaddy, B. (2001). *A handbook for classroom instruction that works.* Alexandria, Virginia: ASCD.

PROCESS: Classroom Observation

 20–40 minutes per teacher

What Is It?

A classroom observation refers to a pre-booked and specified period of time spent in a classroom for the purpose of observing, and usually taking notes, on a specific lesson or segment of a lesson. Observations are always followed by a reflective conversation with the presenting teacher.

Why Do It?

Classroom observations are usually done for one of two purposes—formally, as part of a teacher's performance appraisal, or informally, to coach the teacher. The former is a legal responsibility that belongs solely to the school administrator. The latter can be offered by the administrator, a school coach, a teacher mentor, a district consultant, a teaching colleague, and so on. To these two reasons for classroom observation, I will add a third. If, as school administrator, you have been out of the classroom for a while and missed the experience of explicitly teaching a strategy to students, do yourself the favour of finding a teacher on your staff who works in this way and ask if they would mind if you sat in on a lesson and learned. Strategies are nothing more than plans of action, but when you see an expert teacher show students how to use a plan that allows them to mentally process, organize, and work with information in a new way, and you see the dawning of understanding in students' eyes, it is a similar feeling to spending time in the kindergarten room on a bad day. It will make you feel that all is right with the world and with your school.

When Do You Do It?

Timing depends completely on purpose, as suggested above. To find time, see the suggestions on pages 30 to 32.

Who Does It?

Again, this depends on the purpose. See Why Do It? above.

Steps in Classroom Observation

Since the classroom observation being encouraged in this chapter is that of observing a teacher engaged in explicit teaching of an instructional strategy, the following steps describe what you might expect to see in that situation. The steps are from literacy expert Kylene Beers' (2003, pp. 41–47) description of direct instruction in comprehension strategies, which, with some minor additions, works for any instructional strategy.

1. The teacher will have determined in advance which strategy is going to be modelled and will have thought through why that strategy is particularly important in this situation and which text is going to be most useful in demonstrating the strategy.

2. The teacher tells the students exactly which strategy he or she is going to be teaching, i.e., "While I read this, I am going to be looking for the ways this historical account of women getting the vote in Canada is similar to and different from the account we read yesterday."

3. The teacher then reads the text aloud. A copy of the text is usually projected on a screen so that students can see the teacher marking the text as he or she reads; students may or may not also have their own copy.

4. The read-aloud is accompanied by a think-aloud in which the teacher, while reading, stops frequently to explain what is going through his or her mind in relation to the strategy. In our example, the teacher might say, "Oh, I see from this introductory paragraph that the person telling this account is Nellie McClung, one of the women who advocated so tirelessly for all women to be allowed to vote, whereas the account we read yesterday was by a male newspaper reporter of the time. There's a big difference that I see—not only of gender but, I'm guessing, of perspective. I'll bet I'm going to see lots more differences than similarities between these two accounts, but I'll remember to watch for both."

5. Students are given a guided opportunity to practise the strategy with the teacher's support. In our example, after the teacher has modelled finding and describing several similarities and differences between the texts, he or she might invite students to join in the think-aloud and point out the next examples. Teacher support is gradually withdrawn as students demonstrate competence, at which point they practise the strategy independently, and the teacher monitors. (See Chapter 10, pages 134–139, for more information.) Note that if students are given graphic organizers to use during practise, it is important that the

organizer be one with which they are already familiar. The focus should be on the strategy that is being taught, not on having to learn how to use the graphic organizer (a category of instructional strategies in its own right) as well.

> ## Q & A: CLASSROOM OBSERVATION
>
> **Q: I'm getting lost in the terminology. Is a strategy lesson the same as the mini-lessons I used to give when I was in the classroom?**
>
> A: Mini-lessons are offered for a number of purposes, teaching everything from how to create a science fair backboard to how to use a glossary. Students are encouraged to practise in a mini-lesson, as they are in a strategy lesson, but they move to independent practise more quickly because mini-lessons tend to focus on procedures and skills more than on strategies—there often isn't the same need for guided practise. Strategies may be offered in a mini-lesson, but often by providing a number of examples and stressing connections to students' prior experience, rather than being explicitly taught. Both mini-lessons and explicit strategy lessons are important, but for different reasons.
>
> **Q: Are all strategies teachable? How do you explicitly teach "Reinforcing Effort and Providing Recognition"?**
>
> A: Not all instructional strategies are directed toward students' cognitive skills. Some, like effort and recognition, address students' attitudes and beliefs, which, of course, have a significant bearing on their achievement. A strategy that is focused on attitude can be taught, but not in the explicit manner that has been described.

Learn More About Strategy Terminology

Tompkins, G. (2004). *50 literacy strategies step by step* (2nd ed.). Columbus, Ohio: Pearson Education.

This book is terrific for a busy administrator. It explains 50 commonly used terms, from Anticipation Guides to Writing Groups, in two-page layouts that include grade levels for use, groupings, a description, a step-by-step explanation, applications and examples, and places to go for further information.

TEACHING Adults

An Introduction to the Top Nine Strategies

Significance to student achievement	The chart of instructional categories on page 116 indicates the percentile gain to be expected after teaching and regular use of a strategy.
Common questions and issues	• Doesn't success with a strategy have more to do with a teacher's comfort in using it than with the strategy itself? • How do I do a think-aloud? I've tried them and just feel silly.
When would you use this lesson?	This introduction is not intended to stand alone, but to be linked to your first use of any of the other lessons in this chapter. It is meant to provide context for teachers and a reassurance that the strategy information you are sharing is supported by a careful and thorough analysis of 35 years of research.
Materials you need	Introduction to the Top Nine Strategies PowerPoint presentation and equipment to show it.
Suggested group set-up	Since this lesson will probably be taught in conjunction with Similarities and Differences (see page 124), the group set-up will be choice when teachers enter, then pre-assigned groupings when teachers begin work at the learning centres.

Build the Evidence Base

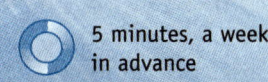

Reflect on whether your staff is familiar with Marzano's research and, if so, whether you need to use this introductory piece. If only some members of staff are aware of his work, use this introduction but perhaps have one or more of the more knowledgeable teachers present it. In that case, request that they also speak to the value of this research in their classroom practice, since hearing the positive experiences of a colleague is highly influential for some teachers.

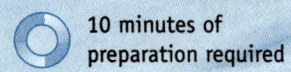

Teach the Session

Have this slide projected as teachers arrive at the workshop. Ask them to talk with the people at their table about what research they are aware of that is known to have an impact on student achievement. Do a quick group share of responses and, when instructional strategies are mentioned, introduce the work of Robert Marzano, formerly a high school English teacher and now Senior Fellow at McREL (Mid-Continent Research for Education and Learning). Mention that he has applied a strategy called meta-analysis, in which the results of a number of studies are combined to determine the average effect of a given strategy, to a review of the last 35 years of educational research.

Explain that Robert Marzano and his colleagues have been able to delineate nine categories of instructional strategies that are proven to have a positive, significant, and measurable impact on student achievement for all students, in all subject areas, and at all grades. Caution teachers that this chart should not be interpreted to suggest that identifying similarities and differences is twice as powerful, for example, as asking good questions. Say that the jury is still out in terms of the usefulness of a particular strategy to a subject, topic, or lesson; that all strategies may not work equally well in all situations or with all students. Remind teachers that knowledge of their students and skill at differentiating instruction is still the best professional action they can take in their classrooms.

Say that one of the top instructional strategies is the identification of similarities and differences, and that metaphor is an example of this strategy. Offer that you have a metaphor for how teachers can think about knowledge of strategies and differentiation. Explain that a non-differentiating teacher with a limited instructional repertoire is similar to a checkers player. In checkers, all playing pieces are the same and the goal is simply to move all of one's pieces from one end of the board to the other, with minimal loss of life. Start the sentence: "Teachers who have a limited instructional repertoire and a generic view of students treat everyone in the same way, with the goal of getting students from September to June…" Pause, and teachers will finish the thought: "…with minimal loss of life."

Now, contrast a checkers player with a chess player. A chess player recognizes the differences among the playing pieces and works with them accordingly. Observe that a chess master has something in the order of 50 000 moves in his or her repertoire. In the same way, a differentiating teacher has a wide range of instructional strategies to apply as needed.

Sustain the Learning

Explicitly acknowledge teachers' learning preferences by providing a variety of ways for them to learn more about powerful instructional strategies. For example:

Hold a book club using Robert Marzano, Debra Pickering, and Jane Pollock's *Classroom Instruction that Works* (2001).

Have a school coach, district consultant, or expert teacher model how to explicitly teach a strategy lesson, or show one of the many videos available for this purpose.

Provide coverage for teachers who would like to observe a strategy lesson taught by a like-grade or like-subject colleague.

Encourage interested teachers to videotape their own strategy teaching for future private or public reflection and analysis.

TEACHING Adults

 40 minutes

SIMILARITIES AND DIFFERENCES

Significance to student achievement	Similarities and differences is a powerful category of instructional strategies because we store information in our brains according to how it is similar and we retrieve it according to how it is different; in other words, according to its critical attributes. The category includes comparison, classification, metaphor, and analogy.
Common questions and issues	• I teach Physical Education, not English. What use are similarities and differences to my subject? • How do you teach someone to compare? Isn't that something people just know how to do?
When would you use this lesson?	This session applies to your entire staff at any point in the school year.
Materials you need	• BLM 9.1 Similarities and Differences Survey (1 per person, in advance of the workshop) • Sheet or two of flipchart paper and marker, or access to a whiteboard or chalkboard • BLM 9.2–9.5— Task Cards (1 per table according to learning centre designation; print on card stock or encase in plastic sleeve to make it clear that this is a task card that should not be removed) • BLM 9.6–9.9—four-quadrant organizers for each of the four centres (1 full set per person, even though they will only have attended two centres) • Work Kit—(1 per table) • Centre materials—see the chart provided in Build the Evidence Base on page 125 • Centre identifiers—tent cards or signs (1 per centre being offered; multiple of a centre if running simultaneously) • BLM 3.2 Workshop Assessment (1 per person, modified for this workshop)
Suggested group set-up	Choice when teachers enter, but will change to pre-assigned groupings when teachers begin work at the learning centres

Build the Evidence Base

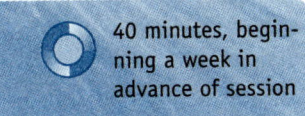 40 minutes, beginning a week in advance of session

Provide teachers with a copy of the Similarities and Differences Survey (BLM 9.1) either at the end of a previous session or at least a week in advance of this session. Collect the forms, determine which centre each person attends first and which second, and note that on the survey form, which you will return to them at the start of the workshop. Each person should be able to attend both of the centres they starred, even if this means that you have multiple "copies" of a centre running simultaneously. If you do have several of one centre, you might want to indicate them as 1A, 1B, and so on on the teacher's survey form with a matching A or B on the centre identifier.

Read the Teach the Session segment completely, then create the centres using the following information as your base:

Centre	Task Card	Materials	Differentiation Possibilities
Comparison	BLM 9.2	A small ball of wool Scissors if needed A number of images randomly torn from magazines or a set of picture cards, typically found in ELL, special education, or primary classrooms	Provide an assortment of word cards related to the teacher's grade level (interest) or of varying degrees of complexity (readiness)
Classification	BLM 9.3	BLM 9.10—Probable Passages—1 per person Copy of a short selection—1 per person in plastic sheet protector	Use different selections—fiction or nonfiction, adult or child—to appeal to teachers' interests. Modify the Probable Passages page accordingly.
Metaphor	BLM 9.4	2 or 3 copies of metaphor bingo boards (BLM 9.11), printed in colour if possible, and encased in a plastic sheet protector	Change the task card to specify the concept to be used (readiness or interest differentiation) or require an extended metaphor—multiple parts—from some teachers (readiness)
Analogy	BLM 9.5	Jeweller's loupes (eyepieces used for examining gems) or small magnifying glasses—1 per person (Note that this activity, rather than producing formally phrased analogies, involves noticing and developing original analogies.)	Provide a variety of small objects—stone, seashell, and so on—for people to look at (interest) or have participants go outside to find the object of their choice (learning preference)

Powerful Instructional Strategies

Learn More About Analogy

Ruef, K. (1992). *The private eye—(5X) looking/thinking by analogy: A guide to developing the interdisciplinary mind.* Seattle, Washington: The Private Eye Project.

This is the best resource I've seen for teaching analogy across the subjects and across the grades. For more information or to order loupes, go to www.the-private-eye.com.

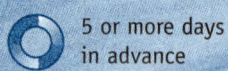 5 or more days in advance

Teach the Session

Return the Similarities and Differences Surveys, with your markings of centres to attend, to teachers as they enter the workshop.

Welcome teachers and tell them that this workshop has been set up so that they will explore the instructional strategy category of similarities and differences by having the opportunity to attend two of four learning stations or centres.

Tell them that learning centres/stations do not necessarily represent differentiated instruction. Invite their thinking as to why this is so (if all students are rotating to all stations and doing the same thing as everyone else at each station, there is no differentiation). Ask teachers to identify what could be done with learning centres to make them differentiated. You may want to record their answers on chart paper. Answers include the following:

- Students attend centres based on interest or need. Teachers are able to provide focused instruction for small groups of students.
- Centres provide multiple ways of working with the material; ways are differentiated according to student interest, need, or learning preference.

State that because you had their pre-assessment information in advance, you were able to set up several examples of a particular centre (name it) because there was interest or need for it and/or you were able to develop materials for each centre according to your knowledge of teachers' interests, needs, or learning preferences.

Teachers sometimes struggle with management concerns around the operation of classroom centres, so take a minute to make your management of the session centres explicit. Point out that the centres were set up when the teachers entered, with the name of each centre clearly indicated, the number of seats at the centre matching the number of participants scheduled to be there, materials ready for the participants, and a task card clearly stating exactly what should be done at the centre. Mention that if papers are in a plastic sleeve it indicates that they should be left at the centre for the next group.

Note that management concerns often arise if the entire class has to sit through an explanation of every centre, and suggest that if task cards don't work—as they won't in some cases—one option is to teach procedures to students one procedure at a time and not add them to centres until they have been taught. You might give Venn diagrams as your example, saying that Venns will be used at the comparison centre, but couldn't be if teachers didn't know what Venn diagrams were and had never worked with them before. Stress that if the focus were on practising using Venn diagrams, the centre content should be familiar to students, but if the focus is to be on new content, the Venn diagrams should be familiar. Another option to handle centre explanations is to teach one student at each centre in advance of the class and have those students function as guides at their respective centres, teaching others and answering questions as needed. As always, students should be invited to provide suggestions for how centre management might be improved.

Invite teachers to suggest other management tips that have worked for them and record their ideas.

This first part of the session should have taken between 10 and 15 minutes, leaving teachers 10 minutes each at 2 centres. Give teachers a set of organizers (BLMs 9.6–9.9) and ask them to move to the first centre you have indicated for them (see Build the Evidence Base on page 125).

Just before signalling for movement to the second centre, make it obvious that you are making another management request and ask that participants return the centre they are at to its original condition.

When both centres have been completed, invite a whole-group debrief of both the process of the centres and the content of the Similarities and Differences work. Explain the next step you would like teachers to take (see Sustain the Learning, below) and ask that participants complete the Workshop Assessment form (BLM 3.2) before leaving.

Powerful Instructional Strategies **127**

Sustain the Learning

Instructional strategies are a perfect opportunity for Schmoker's Rapid Results data analysis mentioned earlier (see Chapter 4, page 53). Ask teachers to create simple pre- and post-assessments before beginning to teach one of the two strategies they explored at the centres. After administering the pre-assessment, teachers work with grade or subject partners to develop a series of lessons that will be implemented over the next month. Have students complete the post-assessment and compare the before and after results. Teachers then meet, in teams or at the next staff workshop, and discuss their results and the methods they used to obtain them. This information then informs the next round of teaching, either of the same strategy or of a new one. Note: If moving on to a new strategy, remember to maintain existing strategies as well, since a single month is not sufficient for many students to master a strategy in all of its various applications.

If you have the entire school working on a strategy together, parents will have, many for the first time, a clear picture of where their child has progressed from and where he or she is going in terms of sophistication of use of a powerful instructional strategy. Share this information in your newsletter by providing a brief explanation of the strategy and its importance, then giving representative tasks from different grade levels along with a sample of student work from each grade.

CHAPTER 10
Appropriate Challenge Through Formative Assessment

CHAPTER AT A GLANCE

Section	Focus	Action/Time
Challenging Your Staff (p. 130)	Administrators and teachers set objectives, provide effective feedback, and use formative assessments to determine next steps	Read
Process (p. 131)	Providing effective feedback	Varying amounts of time, on a frequency determined by you
Teaching Adults (p. 134)	Lev Vygotsky and the zone of proximal development Appropriate challenge in the classroom Multiple entry points to learning	40 minutes plus 10 minutes of preparation for workshop (no preparation required for Build the Evidence Base)
Teaching Adults (p. 140)	Providing feedback	40 minutes, plus 30–60 minutes of preparation a week in advance
Teaching Adults (p. 145)	Formative assessment—assessment *for* and *as* learning	30 minutes, plus 15 minutes of preparation a week in advance

MODEL FOCUS

Appropriate Challenge & Evidence Base

Challenging Your Staff

This chapter focuses on teachers providing the appropriate level of challenge for each learner. To do this, teachers must identify where the learner is now and what actions to take to advance the learning. This means they need to engage in formative assessment, or assessment *for* learning, and, where possible, they need to involve their students in self-assessment, or assessment *as* learning.

The material in this chapter can be challenging for teachers because it is focused on the individual learner and therefore, at first glance, seems overwhelming and time-consuming. However, determining appropriate challenge and scaffolding the learner as he or she progresses is manageable when two conditions are met: teachers must become comfortable using exit cards and other straightforward forms of formative assessment rather than testing, and they must learn to use verbal feedback and student involvement in assessment as learning rather than nonstop marking of assignments. Further, since providing appropriate challenge and effective feedback are indicators of highly effective, differentiating teachers, learning to do both is professionally affirming.

As an administrator, your role with teachers is identical to that of teachers with students. You keep everyone focused on the school-wide goals established in Chapter 4, and provide effective feedback to individual teachers so they know where they are in achievement relative to the goal and the steps they can take to continue to progress. The classroom walk-throughs, workshop assessments, and other processes described in this book are all forms of formative assessment that provide you with the evidence you need to make effective instructional decisions.

Learn More About Formative Assessment

Black, P., Harrison, C., Lee, C., Marshall, B., & Wiliam, D. (2003). *Assessment for learning: Putting it into practice*. New York: McGraw-Hill Education.

This book is an expansion of the well-known article *Inside the Black Box* by the same authors. It is based on a two-year project involving 36 teachers who learned to use formative assessment strategies in their classrooms. School administrators are provided with suggestions for promoting and supporting classroom changes.

Earl, L. (2003). *Assessment as learning: Using classroom assessment to maximize student learning*. Thousand Oaks, California: Corwin Press.

This book clearly explains the differences among assessment for, as, and of learning, and provides helpful case studies and suggestions to support the use of assessment in planning appropriate challenges for students.

PROCESS: PROVIDING EFFECTIVE FEEDBACK

Varying amounts of time, on a frequency determined by you

What Is It?

Effective feedback consists of giving an individual specific comments and suggestions in relation to their achievement of a goal or target behaviour.

When Do You Do It?

Frequency is relative to purpose. A teacher who is being formally assessed for a performance appraisal, for example, may receive more involved and frequent feedback than other teachers. This will certainly be the case if the teacher being assessed is struggling and you are trying to determine whether feedback will result in substantial improvements.

If your purpose is to support teachers as they work toward a school-wide goal, timely feedback offered when teachers are taking actions toward that goal is most useful. You don't need to book full classroom observations for this purpose. If the entire staff is working on an idea from a chapter in this book, you should be able to see a number of teachers in action during a school or classroom walk-through and can provide effective feedback in a two-minute chat during a break in the day.

Why Do It?

Some of the key benefits of effective feedback include the following:

- it underscores the importance of the action for which you are offering comment
- it demonstrates your commitment to effective instruction as being your prime concern
- it provides teachers with progress markers in their achievement of a goal
- it increases teacher learning, and therefore student achievement, because it is timely and specific

Appropriate Challenge Through Formative Assessment

Who Does It?

Anyone can offer feedback. Some teachers will be more receptive to feedback offered by you; others to feedback offered by a peer.

Steps in Providing Effective Feedback

1. Make sure teachers understand the purpose of your observation. They should have a detailed and specific understanding of the goal.

2. Begin with positives. Express admiration and appreciation for what the teacher is doing well relative to the goal. Again, be as specific as possible.

3. Say what you would like the teacher to work on, again relative to the goal. Give information or offer personalized assistance (i.e., suggesting that you will provide coverage so that the teacher can go to Mrs. X's classroom and observe how she handles a particular focus).

4. Thank the teacher for his or her work and express your conviction that they will continue to progress.

Q & A: Effective Feedback

Q: How do I respond to the teachers who are disappointed that I am only commenting on, and therefore only seem to be noticing, part of a lesson?

A: Make sure teachers are aware of the goal before you observe them. Tell them at the start of the feedback session, if not earlier, that for feedback to be effective in terms of its impact on student, or teacher, understanding and actions, it must be specific to a goal or outcome. Explain that you are keen to prevent teacher overload and burnout, so want to focus on only one or two goals at a time.

Q: I am often sidetracked by aspects of a lesson that have nothing to do with the goal. How can I stay focused?

A: Before entering the classroom, make a list of what you might expect to see as evidence of the goal's achievement. Incidentally, the development of these lists is a great activity for an administrators' study group.

Q: This is the instructional leadership action that concerns me. I have been too long out of the classroom to offer specific instructional advice to teachers. Isn't that the role of school coaches and district facilitators?

A: If you are really uncomfortable, it's fine to leave this responsibility to people whose time in the classroom is more recent than yours. Those individuals tend to also have more up-to-date professional knowledge as a result of attending conferences or district training sessions. However, if you are leaving the feedback to others, make sure they have a clear understanding of the school-wide goals. You may want to sit in on a couple of observation and feedback sessions to monitor how they are being handled and to determine if the comments are really all that different from what you would have offered.

Peanuts: © United Feature Syndicate, Inc.

Learn More About Classroom Feedback

Johnston, P. (2004). *Choice words: How our language affects children's learning.* Portland, Maine: Stenhouse Publishers.

The subtitle of this book says it all. Johnston provides examples of questions and statements that encourage the development of students' reflective and strategic thought. The classroom examples in this book are from K–4 classrooms, but most will be useful at all grades.

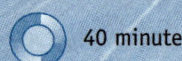

TEACHING Adults

40 minutes

VYGOTSKY AND THE ZONE OF PROXIMAL DEVELOPMENT

Significance to student achievement	The space between what a student can do unaided and what he or she can do with assistance is referred to as the zone of proximal development (ZPD). You might think of it as work that is just a bit more difficult than a student can handle without help. The ZPD is significant to student achievement because it is the situation in which learning occurs.
Common questions and issues	• How do I know a student's zone? • I am the only adult in the room. How can I possibly provide the appropriate level of challenge for every student?
When would you use this lesson?	Defining and providing appropriate challenge is part of the artistry of teaching and not easily or permanently achieved, making this an excellent topic for ongoing exploration in professional learning communities and teaching teams. Since differentiated instruction is based on knowing the strengths and needs of the individual learner and then working to address those needs, appropriate challenge is an important workshop for all staff, but it should come after work on knowing the learner and essential understandings.
Materials you need	• Work Kit—1 per group • Flipchart or board and markers • List of entry points prepared so they can be seen by everyone (i.e., on flipchart or whiteboard) • BLM 1.2 *Success for Every Student* Model (1 to demonstrate or 1 per person)—optional • BLM 10.1 Scaffolding for Instruction in the ZPD (1 per person) • Drawing paper, flipchart size or larger (1 sheet per group) • Small cards, each with a different scenario (see examples in Teach the Session; 1 per group) • BLM 3.2 Workshop Assessment (1 per person, modified for this workshop)
Suggested group set-up	Teacher choice

134 Chapter 10

Build the Evidence Base

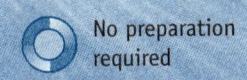
No preparation required

Since all teachers will be able to personalize this workshop to their level of readiness, there is no need to build the evidence base.

You will need to prepare your rendition of the Goldilocks and the Three Bears story.

Teach the Session

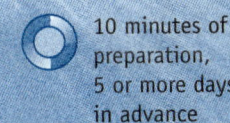
10 minutes of preparation, 5 or more days in advance

You will be presenting this material through a number of entry points. Have a list of the entry points visible on flipchart paper or a whiteboard, but don't refer to it. At the end of the session, you will ask teachers about the entry points that you used.

Entry points to list are the following:

- Narrative (tell a story)
- Logical quantitative (share an organizer, chart, or graph)
- Foundational (discuss the theory)
- Aesthetic (work in an art form)
- Experiential (involve in activity)

One of your goals for this workshop is to show teachers that it can be relatively easy to introduce a concept through multiple entry points, and that it is enjoyable and helpful for the learner to be given more than one way to understand and work with new material. You want teachers to become aware of being bombarded with multiple representations of the same basic concept, so keep the lesson moving quickly.

Tell teachers that today's workshop is about supporting individual students with the appropriate level of challenge to encourage their learning. Point out where Appropriate Challenge is on the *Success for Every Student* model (BLM 1.2), noting that it is both a condition of effectiveness and a component that is differentiated. Observe that Appropriate Challenge, supported by all of the other components, leads directly to Student Achievement. Note that you have to have evidence to create Appropriate Challenge. Point to Evidence Base on the model and note its relationship to Appropriate Challenge, as signified by the double-headed arrow.

Abruptly switch topics, asking teachers if they remember the story of Goldilocks and the Three Bears. You not only are using a narrative entry point but also are creating a hook for the lesson and setting up contrasting experiences of support and rejection, so have fun with this introduction. Read teachers a picture book version of the story, tell the story yourself, have a teacher tell it, or perform it as a puppet show—whatever works for your style. Then, ask teachers what on earth Goldilocks and the Three Bears have to do with appropriate challenge in the classroom. If teachers are momentarily stymied—and they should be with your abrupt changes in topic and approach—tell them it wasn't a difficult question and urge them to think harder.

When someone provides the correct answer—that Baby Bear's "just right" porridge, chair, and bed is akin to providing the "just right" level of challenge and support for the learner—be generous in your praise. Tell them how smart they are, what a good thinker they are, and so on. In contrast, when someone gives an incorrect answer, tell them flatly that their answer is wrong, don't give them any hints or support, just move on to the next person.

Debrief immediately with teachers, asking them what you did that was contradictory to providing appropriate levels of challenge and support, and what you did, if anything, that was appropriate. Record the ideas in a two-column chart with heads such as Appropriate/Inappropriate or Helpful/Not So Much.

Go to the board and draw a circle with a ring around it. Leave enough room so that you can later add two more rings to the outside of your diagram. Explain that this image signifies a theory that is very important to educators, developed by a Russian psychologist by the name of Lev Vygotsky (1978). Ask for a show of hands of anyone who has heard his name. Then ask the people who have their hands raised to keep their hand up if they have more than heard Vygotsky's name; if they could explain his theory to a colleague. Reassure them you won't ask them to do that. If any teachers still have their hands raised, write their names in small print in the inside circle, then label the circle Zone of Actual Development, or ZAD.

Talk about the zone of actual development as being the place where learners can work independently because in that zone they are practising their learning, humming along in their work, and not feeling particularly taxed. The zone of actual development is a great place for being confident about your abilities. Ask teachers to privately settle on a number—the percentage of time students should be "hanging out" in the zone of actual development.

Then say assertively that it is *not* a place where you would like to see students spending most of their time. Explain that the zone of actual development is a great place for consolidation, a great place for a rest, but it is not an ideal place for learning. Write zone of proximal development (or ZPD for short) in the outer ring and emphasize that this is where learning occurs. Say that in this zone the work is just a little bit tougher than students can handle without help. When they receive help and are then able to do something they couldn't do before, that skill becomes internalized and part of their new zone of actual development. Note that if the work is too difficult for a student to do, even with assistance, the only zone that student is in is the frustration zone, and that isn't a productive place to be.

Draw another ring and label it ZAD, explaining that students stay there and independently practise and apply their new skill until they are nudged again into a new zone of proximal development. Draw another ring and label it ZPD. Speaking metaphorically, you might want to comment that, like the giant sequoias in California, we want to grow students with lots of rings.

Tell teachers you can understand that the zone of proximal development would not be a particularly welcome theory if they were imagining that they had to dash from one student to another all day long, diagnosing zones of actual development and pushing and supporting students into new zones of proximal development. Reassure them that direct assistance from them is only one of the many ways students can receive support, or what Vygotsky called *scaffolding*. Give each teacher a copy of BLM 10.1 and ask them to do a private self-assessment, checking all the statements that are true for how students are supported in their classroom and adding any that you might have missed. While teachers are doing this, hand out a large sheet of blank drawing paper to each group.

The activity you will have groups complete is to draw the rings of the ZPD and ZAD for the scenario you will provide on a card. They may start either in a zone of proximal or a zone of actual development and should use images and/or single words to describe the scaffolds that advanced them through the zones. Ask that when groups are finished, they post their drawings on the wall for a gallery walk and whole-group review, including some guessing as to what scenario they were sharing, so not to make the words too obvious. Note that the scenarios involve multiple skills or strategies, whereas in the classroom we think in terms of development of a specific skill. You are providing

Appropriate Challenge Through Formative Assessment **137**

scenarios because teachers may not remember how they learned a specific skill from their childhood.

Say that, in support of choice as the hub of the differentiated instruction wheel, groups are welcome to develop the scenario of their choice, rather than using the one you give them on the card.

Some of the choices to put on the scenario cards could include learning

- to drive a car
- in the first month, of the first year, of teaching
- to differentiate instruction this year
- to use math manipulatives effectively in the classroom
- to work as part of a professional learning community

Distribute the Workshop Assessment (BLM 3.2) while groups are working.

Take a few minutes for the gallery walk. Summarize the learning by asking this question: At the beginning we agreed that Baby Bear's "just right" resources (bed, porridge, chair) were a good metaphor for appropriate challenge. Do you still think that statement is true? Ask for a thumbs up/thumbs down vote, then ask how they would know for sure. If it isn't offered, make the point that we look to the learner to determine whether he or she was in a zone of proximal or actual development. What was Goldilocks doing when the bears arrived home? She was sleeping, which is definitely not a ZPD activity!

Ask teachers to look at the list of entry points you have posted and to notice that in the last 40 minutes, they have been introduced to the zone of proximal development and the concept of appropriate challenge in all five ways. Ask them to complete the Workshop Assessment form (BLM 3.2) before they leave. You may want to add a question to that form about the effectiveness of learning through multiple entry points and whether or not teachers now feel more comfortable using multiple entry points in their classrooms.

Sustain the Learning

Teachers can practise determining a student's zone by observing a number of students as they work on a routine task, such as spelling. During an observation, they should write as quickly as they can, describing what they see, not what they think it means. After completing their observations, teachers meet with colleagues from a number of different grade levels who have also observed during a spelling activity. Teachers review their notes together, trying to determine the behavioural characteristics of students who are in the zone of actual development and using the activity for practice, those who don't need the practice and are bored, and those who can't do the work and are frustrated. Finally, teachers should talk about whether any of their students are in the zone of proximal development for this activity and how they know. Teachers can summarize their learning by creating a flowchart of what they have observed and the implications for next steps in planning and teaching. (See Chapter 10 of *Start Where They Are* for an example of a flow chart.)

Use the language of the zones of proximal and actual development when you are discussing a particular student with a teacher. Encourage teachers to observe in order to accurately diagnose a student's current position and to make it easier to determine next steps.

Ask teachers who have completed the Sustain the Learning activity to write a short article about what parents can do at the various grade levels to scaffold students in their spelling work, reading, learning of multiplication facts, or whatever activity the teachers observed.

TEACHING Adults

Providing Feedback

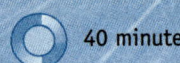
40 minutes

Significance to student achievement	After reviewing 8000 studies, researcher John Hattie concluded, "The most powerful single modification that enhances achievement is feedback" (cited in Marzano et al. 2001, p. 96).
Common questions and issues	• I mark everything my students do on a rubric. Doesn't that give them lots of feedback? • Is it feedback when I tell students that they are doing a good job?
When would you use this lesson?	This lesson is applicable to your entire staff, at any time during the year. Please note that the workshop does involve some role play. Although the role play takes place mostly in partners, with public demonstrations on a completely voluntary basis, you should make sure teachers are comfortable with each other before instructing this session, or modify the way you teach this material.
Materials you need	• BLM 10.2 Quick Write About Feedback (2 copies per person—1 for use before the session and 1 for a couple of weeks after the session) • Listing of teacher concerns about feedback—prepared in advance on flipchart paper—optional • Overhead projector and screen • 6–8 transparencies of student work, some with effective feedback and some with ineffective—see Build the Evidence Base for details • A generic rubric (one that does not provide enough detail to support the student in improving his or her work) • Set of 3 work samples for a single assignment for each grade level in your school—remove student names • An index card per grade level, listing expectations of the assignment for which you have provided work samples
Suggested group set-up	Grade partners

140   Chapter 10

Build the Evidence Base

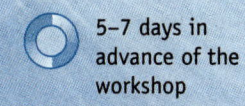
5–7 days in advance of the workshop

Give teachers BLM 10.2 (Quick Write About Feedback) and collect the responses. Unlike BLM 8.1, in which you used self-reports and quick writes to establish learning groups, this pre-assessment allows you to determine what needs to be emphasized in the workshop. You may wish to write up a single-page summary list of teacher concerns for sharing at the workshop.

Distribute copies of the same assessment form (BLM 10.2) several weeks after the workshop and use your comparison of the pre- and post-assessment responses to determine the usefulness of the workshop and next steps for the staff as a whole (or for specific teachers, if you have asked them to put their names on the assessment forms). Do not be surprised if teachers express few concerns in the pre-assessment and numerous concerns in the post. They may believe they are offering effective feedback when they put a mark on a student's paper. When they find out in your workshop that effective feedback is descriptive, not evaluative, personal and management concerns will surface.

Ask willing teachers from each grade level to give you copies of unmarked student work for a single assignment of their choice—one work sample from a student who excels, one from a student who struggles, and one from a student who is in the middle of the continuum. Some of the work can be project material (e.g., dioramas, published student books). In that case you will need originals, not copies. Ask that the teacher give you an index card listing his or her expectations for the assignment.

Remove or mask all student names. Choose six to eight single-page paper assignments from an assortment of grade levels, subject areas, and student levels. Make photocopies and mark some of these photocopies with ineffective feedback and some with effective feedback.

Examples of ineffective feedback include the following:

- checkmarks and Xs with a tally, for example, 6/10
- a letter grade
- a letter grade and a comment such as "Good work!" or "You can do better"

- a comment on a weak piece of work that has nothing to do with the expectation being addressed, for example, "Remember to date your work"

For one of the ineffective pieces, create a simple rubric that uses generic descriptors such as "some, most, all" and circle the student's achievement.

Examples of effective feedback include the following:

- pointing out specific strengths in writing, with or without a letter grade, for example, "Joey, this answer shows that you really know how to summarize!"
- explaining specific weaknesses, pointing out how to revise, and saying you would like the assignment returned to you
- having students look for the errors, for example, "Six of these questions are correct and four are incorrect. I have marked two correct answers and one incorrect one. Please find the other three incorrect responses, correct them, and return to me."

Make transparencies of the selections you have marked. Keep the other selections, and the unmarked photocopies of the transparency selections, for use during the workshop.

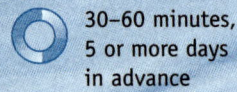
30–60 minutes, 5 or more days in advance

Teach the Session

Welcome teachers and ask them to sit with their grade-level partners.

Tell teachers that this session is about providing effective feedback to students so they know what they are doing correctly, what they are doing incorrectly, and what they need to do as a next step in their learning. You may wish to quickly review teacher concerns about feedback if you have listed those, and to explain what will take place in this workshop.

Thank the volunteering teachers for their student work contributions and make it clear that the marking of assignments was done by you, not the teachers. Project the transparencies one by one, asking teachers to focus on the feedback you have provided (not on the assignment). Have teachers indicate, by a show of hands, whether each selection should go in the effective feedback pile or the ineffective feedback pile. Save the rubric selection for last. This is a concept-attainment lesson in which you are helping teachers identify the critical attributes of effective feedback, so it is important that you put the assignment in the appropriate pile regardless of whether or not teachers voted for it to be there. See Bennett and Rolheiser (2001) for more information about concept attainment.

When all pieces have been sorted, go through each of the two piles again, having a teacher create a two-column chart and recording the group's thinking about what constitutes effective or ineffective feedback. You want them to come to the conclusion that effective feedback gives a student acknowledgment of what's right, help or direction to fix what's wrong, and understanding of what they need to do next. You will know that has been achieved if teachers initially put the generic rubric in the effective feedback pile (we tend to believe that all rubrics are helpful) and then want to change it after your discussion.

Hand out the three samples of work from their grade level to each grade team. If there is only one teacher per grade level, ask them to partner with someone from a nearby grade (e.g., a Grade 7 teacher with a Grade 6 or Grade 8 teacher) and give them the three samples from just one grade level. Ask that teams review the three work samples, providing effective feedback for each. If you delay giving the index cards for a few minutes, you should hear teachers saying that it is difficult to provide effective feedback when they don't know the teacher's expectations. At that point, offer the index cards and the observation that students have the same problem if they are doing work and haven't been told the learning goal or how they will be assessed.

After teachers have had a few minutes to provide the effective written feedback on a selection, ask that they provide the other two feedbacks as role plays in which the student has the assignment in front of him or her and is working on it, and the teacher is stopping by to check on progress. Students can behave as they wish, but you should ask that the teacher in the role play follow these three steps in effective feedback (Marzano et al., 2001):

1) *Tell the student what he or she is doing correctly as it relates to the learning outcome.*

2) *Tell the student what he or she is doing incorrectly as it relates to the learning outcome. Be specific and give new information or an explanation that helps to promote understanding.*

3) *Ask the student to keep working until he or she succeeds.*

Close the session by asking teachers to share with their partner what they found useful about today's workshop and what they will try in their classrooms. Alternatively, if you hear or sense that teachers are concerned that effective feedback will take too much time, close the session by asking teachers to each give one time-saving tip that has worked or they think would work when providing effective written or verbal feedback. When someone says that verbal feedback takes less time than written feedback, offer that this is particularly important because research shows that feedback is far more useful to the learner when it is timely.

Ask teachers to begin or continue to incorporate some of today's workshop ideas into their classroom work. Advise them that you will be giving them another copy of the pre-assessment in a couple of weeks and will look forward to reading their reflections.

Sustain the Learning

The learning from this session is readily and usefully sustained if teachers work in grade groups. Together, they can analyze samples of student work, assist one another in providing effective feedback, and collaboratively create detailed and helpful rubrics for key assignments, along with exemplars of student work that can be shared with next year's classes.

Formative Assessment

Significance to student achievement	Assessment provides what Janet Allen calls "the ongoing redefinition of starting points," making it possible for students to progress to greater levels of achievement.
Common questions and issues	• I need marks for the report card. There is no time to do any assessing that does not count for reports. • Students won't take seriously any assessment activity that does not count.
When would you use this lesson?	This lesson is applicable to your entire staff, at any time during the year. If you are new to the school or do not know your staff's individual concerns about assessment and evaluation, you may wish to use the lesson plan in Chapter 11 (page 152) before this one so that you can better differentiate this lesson according to staff needs. Also, it would be best if you have already taught the lesson on essential curriculum outcomes (Chapter 7, page 92).
Materials you need	• Work Kit—1 per group • Formative Assessment PowerPoint presentation and necessary equipment • Blank sheet of paper (1 per person) • BLM 3.2 Workshop Assessment (1 per person, modified for this session) • Exit card (1 per person)—optional
Suggested group set-up	Teacher choice

Appropriate Challenge Through Formative Assessment

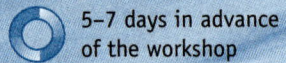

5–7 days in advance of the workshop

Build the Evidence Base

Two concepts are addressed in this session. If you, or members of the planning team, have personal knowledge of teachers' strengths in one of the concepts, you may wish to recruit them to help with part of the session. Alternatively, you may wish to use one of the processes described in this guide to collect information about each staff member's perceptions and practices regarding these two concepts:

- Formative assessments are easier to use for planning if grade books are organized according to outcomes or expectations rather than assignments.

- Exit cards are very helpful in constructing short-term, flexible learning groups.

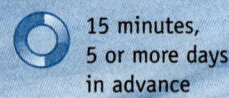

15 minutes, 5 or more days in advance

Teach the Session

Welcome teachers. Say that you would like to ensure everyone has a common understanding of some key terms for the different stages of assessment. Ask them to draw a horizontal line across the middle of a page and put the assessment terms where they belong.

Show the PowerPoint slide to allow teachers to check their work.

Show the quote and invite teachers to talk with a partner to identify the contentious point ("Grading is laid aside") and to summarize the purpose of formative assessment (to help teacher and student identify an appropriate next step in learning). Allow just a couple of minutes for this conversation between partners—long enough for you to get a sense of teachers' feelings and concerns about formative assessment, but not so long that the session goals are derailed by concerns.

Recap the stages of backward design if you have taught the session on essential curriculum outcomes, or introduce them if you haven't (see Chapter 7, page 94). Say that when activities are aligned to goals, when goals and criteria are shared with your students, and when you know what understandings and skills students must have in order to achieve the goals, every activity becomes an opportunity for formative assessment.

If a teacher on staff organizes their grade book according to expectations or outcomes (see Build the Evidence Base on page 146), invite them to speak. If not, show the PowerPoint slide and make the point that when results are entered by assignment, it is impossible for teachers to tell where students need to improve or the steps they can take to help students achieve the learning outcome. However, if results are entered by learning expectations or outcomes, teachers can give specific feedback and make next-step decisions.

Explain that assignments can still be listed under the outcomes because this will provide teachers with more information about what types of assignments work best for each learner.

Observe that formative assessments do not need to be complicated. Describe exit cards as a useful and easy formative assessment strategy. Explain that exit cards are simply half pages with a prompt or question that students respond to in writing during the last few minutes of a class and hand in before they "exit" the classroom at the end of the period. Ask teachers who have experience with exit cards to describe how they use them.

Review the list of sample exit-card prompts and questions.

Explain that exit cards have a couple of important purposes. They are important to differentiated instruction because teachers can group students with similar needs and develop an activity to address those needs. And they are important to effective teaching because well-written exit cards help both teacher and students focus on the essential understanding of the lesson. Students become more aware of what they learn and the conditions under which they learn best. This is the point at which students are engaged in assessment *as* learning, where they reflect on their learning and serve as their own best evaluators.

Ask teachers to think about an upcoming lesson and to write an exit card prompt or question. They can share their question with a partner and discuss possible differentiated activities based on imagined responses to the question.

Conclude the workshop by mentioning that exit cards can be constantly refined. For example, some teachers find that students give more effort to exit cards if the questions are preprinted on coloured paper, perhaps with a border or small image. Other teachers have found that printing the exit cards on paper of various colours has helped them to stay organized when they see multiple groups of students; yellow cards always belong to Mrs. Smith's

Appropriate Challenge Through Formative Assessment

class. Encourage teachers to try out the exit card assessments in their classrooms and to share their experiences.

Ask teachers to complete the Workshop Assessment form (BLM 3.2), or give them a preprinted exit card question, perhaps, "What was crystal clear to you from today's session?"

Sustain the Learning

Interested teachers may wish to work with exit card assessments as an action research project. They can experiment to determine what sorts of questions or prompts provide the most detailed and useful responses and that allow differentiated instruction to occur most readily. Teachers who do this work should be encouraged to share it with others within and beyond the school. There are a number of online action research journals that will be receptive to publishing teacher reports. Writing for an audience is a superior form of professional learning and to be encouraged.

Exit cards are just one of many formative assessment strategies. Teachers can explore others by reviewing district assessment documents, Chapter 10 of *Start Where They Are*, or Lorna Earl's book *Assessment as Learning* (2003). For an in-depth look at self-assessment as it applies to student writing, teachers might be interested in a book study of *Student Self-Assessment* by Graham Foster (1996).

CHAPTER 11

Evaluating Fairly in the Differentiated Classroom

CHAPTER AT A GLANCE

Section	Focus	Action/Time
What Matters? (p. 149)	Specifics of assessment and evaluation in a differentiated classroom	Read
Teaching Adults (p. 152)	Addressing teacher concerns	40 minutes plus 40 minutes of preparation

MODEL FOCUS

Evidence Base

What Matters?

I am convinced that differentiated instruction would be happening in a lot more classrooms if we could just, once and for all, resolve the misconceptions and misunderstandings that exist about assessment and evaluation. Notice that I said "about assessment and evaluation" and didn't add "in the differentiated classroom." This is because when you scratch the surface of a teacher's concern about assessment and evaluation in a differentiated environment, what you usually find is a concern about assessment and evaluation that is true of *any* environment.

There is such a thing as "differentiated assessment," but it is not what most teachers mean when they use the term. What concerns teachers when they talk about differentiated assessment is usually that a mark that is publicly shared (e.g., a mark on a report card), will be relative to each individual student's work and their progress with that work, and therefore will have no meaning. There are so many misunderstandings buried in this concern that it is difficult to know where to begin to untangle them. They include

- mixing assessment (for the purpose of informing instruction and providing descriptive feedback) and evaluation (for the purpose of making a judgment)
- thinking that either assessment or evaluation are norm-referenced when they are in fact criterion-referenced (relative to clearly established criteria to demonstrate achievement of an outcome)
- believing that when students do different assignments in a differentiated classroom, they are working on different outcomes. In fact, the outcomes are not differentiated; it is how the student achieves the outcome that is differentiated
- believing that everything that is marked counts toward evaluation. Formative assessments are assessments *for* learning and are meant to inform next steps for both teacher and student, not to prematurely measure achievement

The legitimate meaning of "differentiated assessment" is that students are given multiple ways to demonstrate achievement of a single learning outcome. Since the outcome is the same for everyone (with the exception of identified students on individual plans), marks and/or comments on the differentiated tasks will all deal with that same outcome. Therefore, the assessment or the evaluation task may be differentiated to enhance the likelihood of achievement for the student by accessing his or her learning strengths or preferences. The final grade, however, if that's what it is being used for, deals with the same criteria and has the same meaning for everyone.

Many concerns about fairness are resolved when teachers understand this concept. Lingering concerns usually relate to one or both of the following ideas:

- Students won't have choice in how they demonstrate their understanding on standardized tests or in high school, college, or life. Is it fair to give them that choice now? Shouldn't we prepare them for the way they are going to have to succeed in the future?
- Written assignments are harder, and more important, than artistic representations or role plays. How is it fair to give two students the same grade when one student wrote a six-page paper and the other made a sculpture?

The first argument again benefits from making the distinction between assessment and evaluation. While students are learning important new work, it makes sense to help them learn that work through a strength. When it comes to evaluation, of course our students have to be prepared to handle written evaluations. No one is suggesting that all evaluations should henceforth be sculpted, danced, or dramatized. But nor does every summative assignment a teacher gives need to make a direct link to the kind of assignment students might receive in college. Talk to teachers about the developmental needs of students in Kindergarten through Grade 8; about the fact that we are preparing them for life, which includes helping them understand themselves as learners and the conditions under which they do their best work; and about that kind of preparation being the best way we can get our students ready for other schools and for their life beyond school.

Peanuts: © United Feature Syndicate, Inc.

The second argument either privileges written responses over other forms of response, or it betrays a teacher's lack of understanding of how to assess other forms. Your response is determined by the reason. If it's the first, take a field trip to an art gallery or studio and have the owner or artist speak to teachers about what is involved in creating art. If it's the second, talk to your art teacher, bring in the appropriate consultants (e.g., media, technology, arts), or invite parents who work in the field to meet with your teachers and teach them how to create alternative assignments that will address the expectations, as well how to assess them.

In the lesson plan that follows, you are encouraged to work with teachers who will help to facilitate small-group discussions about assessment and evaluation. Assessment and evaluation are often sensitive, conflict-generating issues for teachers. By holding conversations in small groups and by gathering information about teacher concerns in advance, you will be able to personalize information about these topics so that your teachers receive the support they need.

Learn More About Assessment and Evaluation

If you'd like a book particularly focused on the differentiated classroom, read:

Wormeli, R. (2006). *Fair isn't always equal: Assessing and grading in the differentiated classroom.* Portland, Maine: Stenhouse Publishers.

For Canadian books about assessment and evaluation in general, have a look at these two titles:

Cooper, D. (2007). *Talk about assessment: Strategies and tools to improve learning.* Toronto, Ontario: Thomson Professional Learning.

Davies, A. (2000). *Making classroom assessment work.* Courtenay, British Columbia: Connections Publishing.

TEACHING Adults

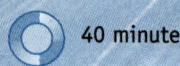

40 minutes

Addressing Teacher Concerns

Significance to student achievement	Summative assessments, or assessments of learning, are evaluations of student achievement. It is important that teachers understand the distinction between evaluations and assessments and are clear about the purposes of each.
Common questions and issues	• How is it fair that two students can both get an "A" although one student only made a diorama while another wrote an essay? • Students will not have their assessment differentiated for them in high school or college. How are we helping them be ready for the real world if we cater to them now? • How will anyone know what a mark means if it's relative to the work of an individual student?
When would you use this lesson?	This lesson is applicable any time of the year, with the entire staff, although perhaps divided into a number of small groups that meet on different days.
Materials you need	• Sticky notes with teacher input before the session, or provocative statements/questions posted for the session • Chairs set in a circle for each group (no tables) and a flipchart or board on which the facilitator will write • Handouts developed by group facilitators (optional)
Suggested group set-up	Teacher choice (see details in Build the Evidence Base on page 153)

Build the Evidence Base

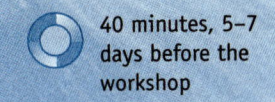
40 minutes, 5–7 days before the workshop

Give each teacher a package of sticky notes (index card size and lined if possible), and ask them to use as many as necessary to write all of their questions and concerns about assessment and evaluation in a differentiated classroom. They should use one note for each comment. Completed notes are to be handed in several days prior to the workshop.

The notes are categorized (e.g., questions and comments about summative assessments, questions and comments about alternative assessments and how to mark them) and a facilitator assigned to each category. Facilitators read over all of the notes in their category and cluster them into like topics so they can create an agenda. Facilitators stay with the topic they have been assigned, but teachers move to new groups two or three times during the workshop.

Here is an alternative to building the evidence base: If you think you know participants' concerns or if you anticipate difficulty in getting them to respond to your request for information, begin a large-group session by posting provocative assessment and evaluation questions or statements around the room. Invite teachers to form groups under the statement that they would most like to discuss first. Tell teachers how many groups they will be able to join during the workshop.

Teach the Session

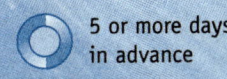
5 or more days in advance

Group facilitators have prepared key messages related to their aspect of the assessment and evaluation discussion, and have checked these key messages with other members of the team.

To determine the key messages, facilitators have

- reviewed teachers' sticky notes to ensure they are clear about teacher concerns and the underlying beliefs and knowledge about assessment and evaluation
- read the section under What Matters? at the beginning of this chapter in order to understand what, if anything, is unique or problematic about assessment and evaluation in a differentiated environment

- made sure they are fully conversant with basic principles and district policies about assessment and evaluation

If teachers are not used to working in groups, norms about shared "air time" and conflict resolution strategies should be discussed with the group before the workshop begins.

Similarly, the purpose of the workshop is determined in advance and shared with participants at the outset. Is the purpose to

- receive key messages and think of applications to the classroom?
- receive key messages and decide whether each person agrees with them or not?
- receive key messages and make a change in practice?
- give teachers an opportunity to share their frustrations and concerns?

Facilitators agree on how to close the workshop appropriately, depending on its purpose. If participants or facilitators feel that another workshop would be helpful, a date is set.

Sustain the Learning

If the group sessions have gone well, continue to offer them either formally, or informally on a monthly drop-in basis.

Use your review of term report cards as an opportunity to have a thrice-yearly discussion about assessment and evaluation with each teacher.

Support teachers working together to design and evaluate assessments.

Do your best to protect teachers from parental concerns about assessment and evaluation in a differentiated classroom by being proactive at every opportunity (e.g., newsletters, meetings, school events) to explain assessment and evaluation practices and the rationale behind them.

CHAPTER 12

Where Are You Now?

School administrators are high-energy people—dedicated and committed professionals who are always reaching for the next—just out of reach—goal, and doing so most often in full view of their staff and school community. There is little to no privacy in the principalship, but sometimes a great deal of loneliness as you try to meet a dizzying array of competing needs and demands, all the while maintaining your composure and your ready smile.

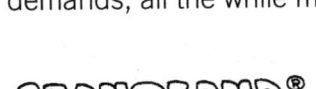

Copyright Grantland Enterprises; www.grantland.net.

We spend so much time identifying everyone else's starting points and shepherding them along that we sometimes forget that, like everyone else, we can only begin from where we are today and move forward into tomorrow. In other words, we need to recognize the complexities of our work and give ourselves a break. When determining where you are now in supporting and sustaining your staff in their efforts to become more effective and more responsive teachers so that students will achieve more, recognize that any new actions you have taken in the midst of a maelstrom of competing priorities are commendable; that where you are now is the best you can do at this moment in time. Take the instructional leadership quiz again (Chapter 2, pages 25–26), or skim through the chapters and jot down a list of what you have done. Then find that minute to reflect, not on all the ways you wish you had done things differently or on all the things left undone, but on the many positive actions you have taken that have moved your school forward and made a difference to staff and students.

Copyright Grantland Enterprises;
www.grantland.net.

If you did the work in

> Chapter 1, teachers learned that a framework or organizing structure helps them to manage their time, feel less overwhelmed and, if the framework is differentiated instruction, be more effective and responsive in their teaching. You used classroom walk-throughs to build a baseline of evidence for two key components of differentiated instruction and you examined the differentiated instruction framework from the perspective of working with your staff.
>
> Chapter 2, you determined your instructional leadership quotient and looked for ways to find time to do this work.
>
> Chapter 3, you reviewed the characteristics of adult learners and examined implications for your work as an instructional leader. You also considered the difficulties in changing people's actions and looked at the

Concerns-Based Adoption Model (CBAM) as a way to provide effective support for teachers at all stages of concern. Finally, you created a workshop assessment form that would allow you to collect formative assessment data to determine next steps in your work with teachers.

Chapter 4, you worked with staff to create a plan for professional learning about differentiated instruction.

Chapter 5, teachers learned about classroom management and organizational procedures that support differentiation, including the need for "withitness" and emotional objectivity to promote positive discipline and build resiliency in students. You examined your role in developing and sustaining strong learning communities and encouraging teachers to be reflective practitioners.

Chapter 6, teachers studied sense-based learning styles, multiple intelligences, student interests, and the important role of choice in motivating students and providing differentiated instruction. You, in turn, looked at staff strengths and how you can acknowledge those and make them central to a positive and supportive school culture.

Chapter 7, teachers were introduced to backward design, to the significance of essential curriculum, and to determining a unit's essential understandings and questions. You reviewed the three responsibilities of an administrator in supporting work on essential understandings: a guaranteed and viable curriculum, understanding of curriculum theory, and resource support.

Chapter 8, teachers studied the vital role of pre-assessments in differentiating instruction, particularly in grouping for learning. You used two pre-assessment structures to determine teacher knowledge and attitude toward pre-assessment so that you could differentiate your workshop on this topic.

Chapter 9, teachers were introduced to Marzano's nine categories of instructional strategies that make a difference to student achievement and received detailed support with the category of similarities and differences. You did classroom observations to watch teachers providing explicit strategy instruction, something you might have missed in your own teaching practice if you have been out of the classroom for a few years.

Chapter 10, teachers learned about the zone of proximal development, multiple entry points to learning, and how to provide effective verbal and written feedback. They also briefly examined formative assessment, specifically how to set up a grade book and how to use exit cards to group students for learning. You examined how to provide effective feedback to staff.

Chapter 11, teachers had an opportunity to address their concerns about assessment and evaluation in general, and about assessment and evaluation in a differentiated classroom in particular. You worked with teachers to clarify that differentiation does not mean individual or unfair assessment practices.

A review of this long list of topics and accomplishments brings me to a second reflection. We need to recognize that learning is the same thing as change and growth. When we approach a teacher in one way and meet with resistance, we learn from that experience and change our approach the next time. The same is true for teachers when they work with students. The question is not, "How do we make the adults in the school become learners?" but rather, "How do we bring learning to the forefront for the adults in the school so they can, on a daily basis, feel the energy and creativity that comes with being actively engaged in learning?" If we could do that, we wouldn't need to give ourselves a break. We would be aware of our learning, we would be aware of our growth, and we would find it easier to be kinder and gentler with ourselves as well as with others.

This reflecting business is helpful. It has taken me an entire administrator's guide to realize it, but I think I can finally articulate the real value of you being an instructional leader. When you take on instructional leadership responsibilities that are new to you, you are consciously aware of your own learning and of your growth. At the same time, you are modelling and supporting both learning and growth in your staff and they, in turn, are providing the same for their students. It is, in Stephen Covey vernacular, a win–win–win situation.

References

Introduction

Cotton, Kathleen. (2003). *Principals and student achievement: What the research says.* Alexandria, Virginia: ASCD.

Chapter 1

Bridges, W. (2001). *The way of transition: Embracing life's most difficult moments.* Massachusetts: Perseus Publishing.

Bridges, W. (2003). *Managing transitions: Making the most of change* (2nd ed.). Massachusetts: Perseus Publishing.

Downey, C., et al. (2004). *The three-minute classroom walk-through: Changing school supervisory practice one teacher at a time.* Thousand Oaks, California: Corwin Press.

Earl, L. (2003). *Assessment as learning: Using classroom assessment to maximize student learning.* Thousand Oaks, California: Corwin Press.

Fullan, M. (2001). *Leading in a culture of change: Being effective in complex times.* San Francisco, California: Jossey-Bass.

Fullan, M., Hill, P., & Crevola, C. (2006). *Breakthrough.* Thousand Oaks, California: Corwin Press.

Hume, K. (2007). *Start where they are: Differentiating for success with the young adolescent.* Toronto: Pearson Education.

Marzano, R. (2003). *What works in schools: Translating research into action.* Alexandria, Virginia: ASCD.

Sosik, J. J., & Dionne, S. D. (1997). Leadership styles and Deming's behavior factors. *Journal of Business and Psychology, 11*(4), 447–462.

Tomlinson, C. A. (1999). *The differentiated classroom: Responding to the needs of all learners.* Alexandria, Virginia: ASCD.

Chapter 2

Blase, J. & Blase, J. (1999). Principals' instructional leadership and teacher development: Teachers' perspectives. *Educational Administration Quarterly, 35*(3), 349–380.

Cotton, K. (2003). *Principals and student achievement: What the research says.* Alexandria, Virginia: ASCD.

Covey, S., Merrill, Roger, & Merrill, Rebecca. (1994). *First things first.* Toronto: Simon & Schuster.

Darling-Hammond, L. (1997). *The right to learn: A blueprint for creating schools that work.* San Francisco, California: Jossey-Bass.

Glickman, C., Gordon, S., & Ross-Gordon, J. (1995). *Supervision of instruction: A developmental approach* (3rd ed.). Boston: Allyn & Bacon.

Haycock, K. (1998). Good teaching matters . . . a lot. *The Education Trust, 3*(2), 3–14.

Lindstrom, P.H., & Speck, M., (2004). *The principal as professional development leader.* Thousand Oaks, California: Corwin Press.

Lovely, S. (2006). *Setting leadership priorities: What's necessary, what's nice, and what's got to go.* Thousand Oaks, California: Corwin Press.

Marzano, R. (2003). *What works in schools: Translating research into action.* Alexandria, Virginia: ASCD.

Marzano, R., Waters, T., & McNulty, B. (2005). *School leadership that works: From research to results.* Alexandria, Virginia: ASCD.

Peterson, K., & Cosner, S. (2005). Teaching your principal: Top tips for the professional development of the school's chief. *Journal of Staff Development,* Spring, *26*(2), 28–32.

Reeves, D. (2004). *Assessing educational leaders.* Thousand Oaks, California: Corwin Press.

Sergiovanni, T. (2007). *Rethinking leadership: A collection of articles* (2nd ed.). Thousand Oaks, California: Corwin Press.

Smith, W., & Andrews, R. (1989). *Instructional leadership: How principals make a difference.* Alexandria, Virginia: ASCD.

References (continued)

Chapter 3

Fullan, M. (2001). *Leading in a culture of change: Being effective in complex times.* San Francisco, California: Jossey-Bass.

Gardner, H. (2006). *Changing minds: The art and science of changing our own and other people's minds.* Boston, Massachusetts: Harvard Business School Press.

Guskey, T. (2000). *Evaluating professional development.* Thousand Oaks, California: Corwin Press.

Hall, G., & Hord, S. (2001). *Implementing change: Patterns, principles, and potholes.* Boston, Massachusetts: Allyn & Bacon.

Holloway, K. (2003). A measure of concern: Research-based program aids innovation by addressing teacher concerns. *Tools for Schools,* Feb/March.

Hord, S. M., Rutherford, W. L., Huling, L., & Hall, G. E. (2006). *Taking charge of change* (Revised ed.), Austin, Texas: SEDL.

Senge, P. M., Kleiner, A., Roberts, C., Ross, R. B., & Smith, B. J. (1994). *The fifth discipline fieldbook: Strategies and tools for building a learning organization.* New York: Currency Doubleday.

Chapter 4

Bernhardt, V. (2002). *The school portfolio toolkit: A planning, implementation, and evaluation guide for continuous school improvement.* Larchmont, New York: Eye on Education.

Bernhardt, V. (2004). *Data analysis for continuous school improvement* (2nd ed.). Larchmont, New York: Eye on Education.

Childs-Bowen, D. (2006). If you build teacher leadership, they will come. *The Learning Principal,* November, Oxford, Ohio: National Staff Development Council.

Conzemius, A., & O'Neill, J. (2002). *The handbook for SMART school teams.* Bloomington, Indiana: National Education Service (now Solution Tree).

Easton, L. B. (Ed.). (2004). *Powerful designs for professional learning.* Oxford, Ohio: National Staff Development Council.

Guskey, T. (2000). *Evaluating professional development.* Thousand Oaks, California: Corwin Press.

Holcomb, E. (2001). *Asking the right questions: Techniques for collaboration and school change* (2nd ed.). Thousand Oaks, California: Corwin Press.

Holcomb, E. (2004). *Getting excited about data: Combining people, passion, and proof to maximize student achievement* (2nd ed.). Thousand Oaks, California: Corwin Press.

Joyce, B., & Showers, B. (2002). *Student achievement through staff development* (3rd ed.). Alexandria, Virginia: ASCD.

Kouzes, J., & Posner, B. (1987). *The leadership challenge.* San Francisco, California: Jossey-Bass.

Palmer, P. (1998). *The courage to teach: Exploring the inner landscape of a teacher's life.* San Francisco, California: Jossey-Bass.

Schmoker, M. (1999). *Results: The key to continuous school improvement.* Alexandria, Virginia: ASCD.

Chapter 5

Benard, B. (2004). *Resiliency: What we have learned.* San Francisco: WestEd.

Blankstein, A. (2004). *Failure is not an option: Six principles that guide student achievement in high-performing schools.* Thousand Oaks, California: Corwin Press.

Chapman, C., & King, R. (2005). Eleven practical ways to guide teachers toward differentiation (and an evaluation tool). *Journal of Staff Development,* Fall, *26*(4), 20–25.

DuFour, R., & Eaker, R. (1998). *Professional learning communities at work.* Bloomington, Indiana: National Education Service.

Eaker, R., DuFour, R., & DuFour, R. (2002). *Getting started: Reculturing schools to become professional learning communities.* Bloomington, Indiana: National Education Service.

Easton, L. B. (Ed.). (2004). *Powerful designs for professional learning.* Oxford, Ohio: National Staff Development Council.

Fullan, M., & Hargreaves, A. (1996). *What's worth fighting for in your school* (2nd ed.). New York: Teachers College Press.

Martin-Kniep, G. (2004). *Developing learning communities through teacher expertise.* Thousand Oaks, California: Corwin Press.

Marzano, R. (2003). *What works in schools: Translating research into action.* Alexandria, Virginia: ASCD.

National Staff Development Council (2007). Time: Find it, save it, stretch it, reshape it [special issue on time management]. *Journal of Staff Development,* Spring, *28*(2).

Palmer, P. (1998). *The courage to teach: Exploring the inner landscape of a teacher's life.* San Francisco, California: Jossey-Bass.

Sergiovanni, T. (1994). *Building community in schools.* San Francisco, California: Jossey-Bass.

Chapter 6

Buckingham, M. (2005). *The one thing you need to know . . . about great managing, great leading, and sustained individual success.* New York: Free Press, a division of Simon & Schuster.

Buckingham, M. & Clifton, D. (2001). *Now, discover your strengths.* New York: Free Press, a division of Simon & Schuster.

Buckingham, M., & Coffman, C. (1999). *First, break all the rules: What the world's greatest managers do differently.* New York: Simon & Schuster.

Kittle, P. (2005). *The greatest catch: A life in teaching.* Portsmouth, New Hampshire: Heinemann.

Liesveld, R., & Miller, J. (2005). *Teach with your strengths: How great teachers inspire their students.* New York: Gallup Press.

Sternberg, R. (2006). Recognizing neglected strengths. *Educational Leadership, 64*(1), 30–35.

Chapter 7

Chapman, C., & King, R. (2005). Eleven practical ways to guide teachers toward differentiation (and an evaluation tool). *Journal of Staff Development,* Fall, *26*(4), 20–25.

Marzano, R. (2003). *What works in schools: Translating research into action.* Alexandria, Virginia: ASCD.

McTighe, J., & Wiggins, G. (2004). *Understanding by design professional development workbook.* Alexandria, Virginia: ASCD.

Wiggins, G., & McTighe, J. (2005). *Understanding by design* (2nd ed.). Alexandria, Virginia: ASCD.

Chapter 8

Marzano, R. (2004). *Building background knowledge for academic achievement.* Alexandria, Virginia: ASCD.

Marzano, R., & Pickering, D. (2005). *Building academic vocabulary* (teacher's manual). Alexandria, Virginia: ASCD.

Chapter 9

Beers, K. (2003). *When kids can't read, what teachers can do: A guide for teachers 6–12.* Portsmouth, New Hampshire: Heinemann.

Marzano, R. (2003). *What works in schools: Translating research into action.* Alexandria, Virginia: ASCD.

Marzano, R., Norford, J., Paynter, D., Pickering, D., & Gaddy, B. (2001). *A handbook for classroom instruction that works.* Alexandria, Virginia: ASCD.

Marzano, R., Pickering, D., & Pollock, J. (2001). *Classroom instruction that works: Research-based strategies for increasing student achievement.* Alexandria, Virginia: ASCD.

Ruef, K. (1992). *The private eye—(5X) looking/thinking by analogy: A guide to developing the interdisciplinary mind.* Seattle, Washington: The Private Eye Project.

Tompkins, G. (2004). *50 literacy strategies step by step* (2nd ed.). Columbus, Ohio: Pearson Education.

Chapter 10

Bennett, B., & Rolheiser, C. (2001). *Beyond Monet: The artful science of instructional integration.* Ajax, Ontario: Visutronx.

Black, P., Harrison, C., Lee, C., Marshall, B., & Wiliam, D. (2003). *Assessment for Learning: Putting it into practice.* New York: McGraw-Hill Education.

Earl, L. (2003). *Assessment as learning: Using classroom assessment to maximize student learning.* Thousand Oaks, California: Corwin Press.

References (continued)

Foster, G. (1996). *Student self-assessment: A powerful process for helping students revise their writing.* Markham, Ontario: Pembroke Publishers.

Johnston, P. (2004). *Choice words: How our language affects children's learning.* Portland, Maine: Stenhouse Publishers.

Marzano, R., Pickering, D., & Pollock, J. (2001). *Classroom instruction that works: Research-based strategies for increasing student achievement.* Alexandria, Virginia: ASCD.

Vygotsky, L. S. (1978). *Mind in society* (M. Cole, V. John-Steiner, S. Scribner, & E. Souberman, Eds.). Cambridge, Massachusetts: Harvard University Press.

Chapter 11

Cooper, D. (2007). *Talk about assessment: Strategies and tools to improve learning.* Toronto, Ontario: Thomson Professional Learning.

Davies, A. (2000). *Making classroom assessment work.* Courtenay, British Columbia: Connections Publishing.

Wormeli, R. (2006). *Fair isn't always equal: Assessing and grading in the differentiated classroom.* Portland, Maine: Stenhouse Publishers.

Glossary

Note: Terms highlighted in blue are structures that are frequently used by teachers who differentiate instruction.

Assessment as learning—students assess their own work and reflect on their growth as learners (see *formative assessment*)

Assessment for learning—assessments that are used to inform instruction (see *diagnostic assessment*, *pre-assessment*, and *formative assessment*)

Assessment of learning—end-of-lesson or end-of-unit assessment (see *summative assessment*)

Authentic assessment—assessment that is relevant to how the student learned the material

CBAM—acronym for Concerns-Based Adoption Model—Hall and Hord, 1987; a model of the process of change for an individual

Choice board—a grid with a variety of activities; a differentiation structure

Constructivism—instructional approach that says learners are actively engaged in using past experiences and constructing knowledge

Cooperative learning—structured group activities built around five elements: positive interdependence, individual accountability, interactive skills, face-to-face interaction, and group processing

Critical attribute—a significant aspect of a concept that defines or helps to define it and differentiate it from all others

Cubing—an activity making use of a cube with questions or activities on each face; a differentiation structure

Declarative knowledge—facts, information, concepts

Diagnostic assessment—assessment used before planning a unit to determine what students already know, understand, and are able to do

Differentiated instruction—a comprehensive framework of effective instruction that is responsive to the diverse learning needs and preferences of individual learners; also known as *responsive instruction*

Effective—having a powerful, impressive impact (in education, the impact is on student achievement)

Emotional objectivity—ability to care without the expectation of a positive response in return

Entry points—ways in which a teacher can introduce new material to students and students can work with that material; multiple entry points give students multiple representations of the same core ideas

Essential questions—big questions based on big ideas/essential understandings. They have no single or obvious right answer, ignite curiosity, lend themselves to multidisciplinary study, are central to a discipline's big ideas, and are worded to engage student interest.

Essential understandings—big ideas essential for all students; they are not differentiated

Evidence base—*all* the ways a teacher makes decisions, including reflection, knowledge of individual students and observation, as well as the full range of formal and informal assessments

Exit cards—an assessment tool; students respond to a prompt on a card and hand it in at the end of a lesson; teachers use information on cards to design instructional activities and to group students for learning

Explicit instruction—teacher-provided intentional modelling or demonstration of a skill or strategy, followed by an opportunity for the student to practise and apply the new learning with teacher support, guidance, and feedback

Flexible grouping—temporary, short-term learning groups based on student interests, readiness, or learning preferences

Formative assessment—assessment during the learning; provides teacher and students with information about student understanding; also known as *assessment for learning*

Heterogeneous group—random selection rather than specific criteria such as academic achievement

Homogeneous group—a group based on specific criteria; an ability group is homogeneous

Inquiry learning—students actively engaged in development of new knowledge through a combination of reading, writing, viewing, discussing, experimenting, and discovering; often the inquiry is in response to essential questions

Instructional approach—the teaching method used during part of or throughout an entire unit (see *inquiry learning*, *project-based learning*, *cooperative learning*)

Integrated learning—when students work on a concept through a variety of disciplines

Intelligences—formats in how the mind thinks; Sternberg says there are three; Gardner says eight or nine

Knowledge of students—a teacher's understanding of each individual student's interests, learning preferences, and readiness to learn a particular concept

Learning community—a group of people focused on the collective goal of learning

Glossary (continued)

Learning preferences—individual differences based on a person's learning styles, intelligences, interests, gender, culture, etc.

Learning station—a place in a classroom where material is collected so that students can work on a specific topic or skill

Learning styles—often, although not always, four categories describing significant ways in which individuals differ in how they learn best; how we prefer to acquire, process, and remember new information

Lesson design—organization and sequence of a lesson or series of lessons in order to create learning experiences that result in maximum student engagement and achievement

Mental model—our beliefs and assumptions

Meta-analysis—a statistical process whereby the results of a number of studies are combined to determine the average effect of a given strategy

Metacognition—reflecting on one's own thinking and learning processes

Multiple intelligences—Howard Gardner's theory that we have nine intelligences, not just one

Multiple representations—variety of ways that students can demonstrate learning or that you can provide new information; corresponds to entry points

Powerful instructional strategies—the research-based strategies proven to have a significant, positive, and demonstrable impact on student achievement

Pre-assessment—assessment used before planning a unit to determine a student's knowledge, understanding, and readiness to learn a new concept; also known as *diagnostic assessment* or *assessment for learning*

Problem-based learning—students are provided with a believable problem that requires acquisition of new knowledge in order to find a solution

Procedural knowledge—processes, strategies, and skills

Procedure—way of doing something in the classroom

Project-based learning—students are assigned authentic, real-life tasks that they investigate over an extended period of time

RAFT—a differentiation structure where students choose the role, audience, format, and topic for an assignment

Readiness—a student's academic starting point; varies by concept

Reliability—consistency, stability, and dependability of results; a reliable result shows a similar performance at different times or under different conditions

Resiliency—ability to bounce back, to regain functioning, after adversity

Respectful task—all students are given tasks that are equally interesting, engaging, and important; tasks respect the learning needs of each student

Routine—a sequence of procedures

Rubric—an assessment tool with a multi-level measurement scale, descriptors for the characteristics of each level, and criteria based on the objectives of an assignment

Strategy—plan of action for processing, organizing, and working with information

Strengths-based revolution—hope that we are going to start paying more attention to individuals' strengths than to their weaknesses

Summative assessment—assessment at the end of a lesson or unit; documents student performance, provides basis for assigning grades; also known as *assessment of* learning; see also *evaluation*

Teacher efficacy—the belief that teachers can influence how well students learn, even difficult or unmotivated students

Think-aloud—verbalization of the thinking process when working through a piece of text or a concept

Tiering—providing different levels of an activity to meet the different levels of student readiness for the concept being taught

Validity—a measure of how well an assessment measures what it is intended to measure

Withitness—the quality of being fully present in the classroom, aware of all students, and able to manage a number of tasks simultaneously

Zone of actual development—where a student is able to work capably and independently, is not taxed, and feels confident about his or her abilities

Zone of proximal development—where a student feels the work is a bit tougher than he or she can handle without help; a term coined by Lev Vygotsky; also known as the *zone of instruction*

Index

A

ability groups, 106–107, 111
acknowledging staff strengths, 75–76
acknowledgment notes, 76
addressing teacher concerns, 152–154
administrators
    see also principals
    and instructional leadership, 24
    principal as instructional leader, 21–24
    role of, in learning community, 61–62
    role with teachers, 130
adult learners
    changing minds, 35–38
    dealing with resisters, 36–37
    described, 33–35
    necessary connections, 34–35
    self-rating as learners, 45
    supporting change, 39–42
Allen, Janet, 145
Andrews, R., 26n
anonymity, 45, 107
appreciation, 76
appropriate challenge
    effective feedback, 131–133
    formative assessment, 129–130, 145–148
    overview, 130
    providing feedback, 140–144
    Vygotsky and the zone of proximal development, 134–139
Arter, Judith, 7
assessment
    see also evaluation
    diagnostic assessment, 6–7, 101–102
    differentiated assessment, 149–151
    and differentiated instruction, 6–7
    vs. evaluation, 150–151
    formative assessment, 7, 129–130, 145–148
        see also appropriate challenge
    of learning, 7
    practices, 6
    pre-assessment, 7, 53, 101–102
    standardized tests, 107
    strengths-finder assessment, 73
    student progress reports, 6
    summative assessment, 7
    workshop assessments, 43–46
Assessment as Learning (Earle), 148
attitude, 101–102, 120
auditory learners, 78

B

background knowledge, 112–114
backward design, 94, 146
Beers, Kylene, 119
being visible, 32
below-standard teachers, 20
Bennett, B., 143
Bennett, Sherrin, 36
Bernhardt, Victoria, 51–52, 53
Black, P., 130
Blase, J., 26n
Bridges, William, 12
Brown, Juanita, 36
Buckingham, Marcus, 71–72, 74
building trust, 12

C

change
    changing minds, 35–38
    supporting change, 39–42
Chapman, C., 67, 96
Chappuis, Jan, 7
Chappuis, Stephen, 7
Chekhov, Anton, 55
Childs-Bowen, Deborah, 54
classroom centre management, 65–66, 126–127
classroom feedback, 131–133
Classroom Instruction that Works (Marzano, Pickering and Pollock), 117, 123
classroom management procedures, 63–65
classroom observation, 118–120
classroom walk-throughs, 17–20
Clifton, Donald, 71–72
Coffman, Curt, 71–72
coherence-making, 3
collaborative teams, 49-50
community. *See* learning community
comprehensive curriculum review, 95–96
concept attainment, 142–143
Concerns-Based Adoption Model (CBAM), 37, 39–40, 58, 104
connections, 34–35, 66
Conzemius, A., 49, 50, 55, 56
Cooper, D., 151
Cosner, S., 28
Cotton, K., 21, 22, 26n
Covey, Stephen, 30, 31
Crevola, C., 3
Csikszentmihalyi, M., 72
cubing, 85
cultural leadership force, 23
curriculum
    comprehensive curriculum review, 95–96
    essential curriculum, 86, 94
    essential curriculum outcomes, 89–90, 92–96
    guaranteed and viable curriculum, 90
    holiday curriculum, 92

D

Darling-Hammond, Linda, 21, 49
data, 50–53
Davies, A., 151
demographics, 51
diagnostic assessment, 6–7, 101
differentiated assessment, 149–150
differentiated instruction
    and assessment, 6–7
    classroom management procedures, 63–65
    "coherence-making," 3
    effective instruction framework, 2–3
    and evaluation, 6–7
    evidence base, 11–12
    focus on, 2–3
    framework, 4–5
    grouping for learning, 106–107
    knowing your learners, 7
    misconceptions, 8
    organizational procedures, 63–65

Index (continued)

resources, 10
Teaching Adults session, 9–16
Tomlinson's model of, 5
what it is, 9–10
differentiation, 5
Dionne, S.D., 12
district-level consultants, 24
dotmocracy process, 57
Downey, C., 20
DuFour, Richard, 34, 61
dysfunctional mental models, 36

E

Eaker, R., 61
Earl, Lorna, 7, 130, 148
Easton, L.B., 48, 49, 70
educational leadership, 22
educational leadership force, 23
effective classroom management, 64, 68
effective feedback, 131–133
effective learning community, 60
effective teaching, 5, 29
80/20 rule, 29
Einstein, Albert, 22
Emerson, Ralph Waldo, 70
emotional objectivity, 67
encouraging reflection, 69–70
entry points, 84–85
essential curriculum, 86, 94
essential curriculum outcomes, 90, 92–96
essential goals, 95
essential understandings, 4, 5, 89–91, 97–100
evaluation
see also assessment
addressing teacher concerns, 152–154
vs. assessment, 150–151
differentiated assessment, 149–150
and differentiated instruction, 6–7
fair evaluation. See fair evaluation
professional learning, 43–46
evidence base, 5, 6, 11–12, 16
exit cards, 146, 147–148

F

feedback, 7, 76, 131–133, 140–144
filing system, 31
flow, 72
follow-up activities, 48
formative assessment, 7, 129–130, 145–148
see also appropriate challenge
Foster, Graham, 148
Fullan, Michael, 3, 34, 60–61n

G

Gaddy, B., 117
Galbraith, John Kenneth, 36
Gallup organization, 71, 73, 76
Gardner, Howard, 37–38, 83–84
Garmston, Robert, 34
Glickman, C., 26n
goal-setting, 51–52, 55–56
Goldilocks problem, 94
Gordon, S., 26n
graphic organizers, 57
group for learning, 106–107, 108–114
guaranteed and viable curriculum, 90
Guskey, Thomas, 43, 45, 48

H

Hall, G., 40n, 42
Hargreaves, A., 60–61n
Harrison, C., 130
Hattie, John, 140
Haycock, K., 21
hierarchy of needs, 63
Hill, P., 3
Holcomb, Edie, 52, 56
holiday curriculum, 92, 93
holidays, 88
Hord, Shirley, 40n, 41, 42, 61
Huling-Austin, L., 40n
human leadership force, 23

I

individual differences, 77–81
ineffective feedback examples, 141–142
ineffective practices, 19–20
inquiry-based learning, 90–91
instructional leadership
administrators, effect on, 24
effective feedback, 133
improvement of student achievement, 35–36
misconceptions, 24
plan for instructional leadership, 31
principal as instructional leader, 21–24
as priority, 29–31
quiz, 25–28
realistic and achievable vision of, 24
supporting and sustaining teachers, 39–42
time drains, identifying and dealing with, 32
instructional strategies. See powerful instructional strategies

J

Johnston, P., 133
Journal of Staff Development, 62
journals, 70
Joyce, B., 48

K

Killion, 70
kinesthetic learners, 77, 78
King, R., 67, 96
Kittle, Penny, 88
knowing-doing gaps, 27–28
knowledge of students
background knowledge, 112–114
interests, 5
learning preferences, 5
pre-assessment, 101–102
pre-assessment to group for learning, 106–107
readiness to learn, 5

strengths revolution, 71–74
summary of, 12
knowledge of teachers
see also adult learners
acknowledging staff strengths, 75–76
interests, 5
learning preferences, 5
readiness to learn, 5
strengths revolution, 71–74
Koch, Richard, 29, 41
Kounin, Jacob, 67
Kouzes, J., 50

L

leadership forces, 22–23
Leadership Forces Hierarchy, 22
learner, aspects of, 5
learning community
administrators' role, 61–62
characteristics of, 59–61
effective learning community, 60
encouraging reflection, 69–70
strength of, 5
summaries of, 12
supports for, 61–62
learning designs, powerful, 49
learning preferences research, 70
learning styles, sense-based, 77–81
Lee, C., 130
Levin, James, 69
Lezotte, Larry, 51, 52
Liesveld, R., 74
Lindstrom, P.H., 24
LOPI (Levels of Program Implementation), 104
Lovely, S., 27, 27n

M

management concerns, 126–127
Marshall, B., 130
Martin-Kniep, G., 60
Marzano, Robert, 9, 16, 21, 26n, 29, 62, 90, 114, 116, 117, 121–122, 123, 143

Maslow, Abraham, 63
McNulty, B., 26n
McREL (Mid-Continent Research for Education and Learning), 122
McTighe, Jay, 45, 90, 91, 94, 98, 99, 100
meetings, 32
mental models, 34, 36
mental surgery, 37–38
Merrill, Rebecca, 30
Merrill, Roger, 30
meta-analysis, 122
Miller, J., 74
mind-changing methods, 35–38
mini-lessons, 120
misconceptions
about differentiated instruction, 8
about instructional leadership, 24
Mizell, Hayes, 21, 44
modelling, 38
multiple intelligences, 82–86
multiple intelligences theory, 70

N

National Staff Development Council, 48, 49
negative behaviours, 66
non-compliance, 105–106
nonstop activity, 32
Norford, J., 117

O

"one-legged" interview, 41
O'Neill, J., 49, 50, 55, 56
open-door policy, 32
optional alternate ending, 15–16
organizational procedures, 63–65
organize around your priorities, 31

P

Palmer, Parker, 49, 60, 69

Pareto, Vilfredo, 29
Pareto Principle, 29
Paynter, D., 117
perceptions, 52
performance appraisal, 20
Peterson, K., 28
Pickering, Debra, 114, 116 n, 117, 123
plan for instructional leadership, 31
Pollock, Jane, 116 n, 117, 123
positive power of groups, 37
Posner, B., 50
potentials, 84
Powerful Designs for Professional Learning (Easton), 48, 70
powerful instructional strategies, 5, 16
categories affecting student achievement, 116
classroom observation, 118–120
influence on community development, 5
overview, 115–117
similarities and differences, 124–128
strategy terminology, 120
top nine strategies, introduction to, 121–123
powerful learning designs, 49
pre-assessment, 7, 53, 101–102, 103–107
pre-assessment to group for learning, 108–114
principal-teacher, 22
principals
see also administrators; instructional leadership
finding time, 29
as instructional leader, 21–24
instructional leadership quiz, 25–28
preparation programs, 27–28
prioritizing responsibilities, 29–32
priorities
organize around your priorities, 31
prioritizing responsibilities, 29–32
processes
acknowledging staff strengths, 75–76
classroom observation, 118–120
classroom walk-throughs, 17–20
effective feedback, 131–133

Index (continued)

encouraging reflection, 69–70
pre-assessing teacher knowledge, 103–107
professional learning plan, 54–58
workshop assessments, 43–46
professional learning
    evaluation of, 43–46
    goal, establishment of, 51–52, 55–56
    high-quality professional learning, 48
    overview, 47–48
    plan for, 54–58
    progress markers, 52–53
    staff meetings, 48
    working with data, 50–51
profiles, 84
progress markers, 52–53
providing feedback, 140–144

Q

quick writes, 103–107

R

"Rapid Results" structure, 53, 128
Reeves, Doug, 27
reflection, 69–70
reflective conversations, 70
resisters, 36–37
risk-taking behaviours, 38
Rolheiser, C., 143
Ross-Gordon, J., 26*n*
Round-Robin discussions, 37
routine tasks, 32
Ruef, K., 126
Rutherford, W., 40*n*

S

Sallee, Marguerite, 38, 52
scaffolding, 137
Schmoker, Mike, 53, 55, 128
school-based coaches, 24
school effectiveness research, 62
school processes, 52
self-rating scale, 45
self-reflection, 38
self-reports, 103–107
Senge, P.M., 36
sense-based learning styles, 77–81
Sergiovanni, Thomas, 22, 23*n*, 60
Showers, B., 48
similarities and differences, 124–128
SMART goals, 55, 56, 57
Smith, W., 26*n*
Sosik, J.J., 12
Speck, M., 24
staff strengths, 75–76
standardized tests, 107
Start Where They Are, 15, 68, 148
Sternberg, Robert, 82, 83–84
Stiggins, Richard, 7
"Stopping at a Lunchroom Table" (Kittle), 88
strategies. *See* powerful instructional strategies
strategy lesson, 120
strategy terminology, 120
strengths-finder assessment, 73
strengths revolution, 71–74
student achievement goal, 35–36, 37
student interests, 87–88
student learning, 51
student progress reports, 6
Student Self-Assessment (Foster), 148
student strengths, 71–74
Success for Every Student/Teacher model
    see also differentiated instruction
    as double diamond, 14
    essential understandings, 98
    evidence base, 6
    the framework, 4–5
    teach the session, 13–15
summarizing teacher beliefs, 12
summative assessment, 7
supporting change, 39–42
supporting teams, 49–50
survey, 40–41
symbolic leadership force, 23
systematic review process, 91

T

tactile learners, 78
tardiness, 32
teacher leaders, 54
teacher presence, 66–68
teachers
    see also adult learners
    acknowledging staff strengths, 75–76
    addressing teacher concerns, 152–154
    pre-assessing teacher knowledge, 103–107
    quality, 21–22
    resistance, 19
    resisters, 36–37
    supporting and sustaining, 39–42
    understanding of, 58
Teaching Adults
    addressing teacher concerns, 152–154
    classroom management and organizational procedures, 63–65
    essential curriculum outcomes, 92–96
    essential understandings and questions, 97–100
    formative assessment, 145–148
    individual differences and sense-based learning styles, 77–81
    lesson plans, 34, 48
    multiple intelligences, 82–86
    providing feedback, 140–144
    sessions, 37, 44
    similarities and differences, 124–128
    student interests, 87–88
    teacher presence, 66–68
    top nine strategies, introduction to, 121–123
    using pre-assessments to group for learning, 108–114
    Vygotsky and the zone of proximal development, 134–139
    what is differentiated instruction, 9–16
technical leadership force, 22
textbook purchases, 91
time drains, 32
time management, 17, 62, 75, 76
Tomlinson, Carol Ann, 5

Tompkins, G., 120
triarchic intelligence model, 82
trust, 12
Twain, Mark, 27
"tyranny of the urgent," 30

U

Understanding by Design Professional Development Workbook (Wiggins and McTighe), 100
Understanding by Design (Wiggins and McTighe), 90, 94, 100
unexpected visitors, 32
unit planning, 94

V

visibility, 32
visitors, unexpected, 32
visual learners, 78
Vygotsky, Lev, 134–139

W

walk-throughs, 17–20
Waters, T., 26*n*
Wellman, Bruce, 34
Wiggins, Grant, 90, 91, 94, 98, 99, 100
Wiliam, D., 130
"withitness," 67, 68
work kit, 10, 31
working with data
    goal, establishment of, 51–52, 55–56
    overview, 50–51
    progress markers, 52–53
workshop assessments, 43–46
Wormeli, R., 151
written acknowledgments, 75–76

Y

Young, Paul, 30

Z

Ziggy cartoon, 99
zone of proximal development, 134–139

Credits

P. x, CORNERED © 2006 Mike Baldwin. Reprinted with permission of UNIVERSAL PRESS SYNDICATE. All rights reserved; **p. 2**, Shutterstock; **p. 3**, Copyright 2004 by Randy Glasbergen, www.glasbergen.com; **pp. 22–23** (pyramid and table), Adapted from Sergiovanni, Thomas (2007). *Rethinking Leadership: A Collection of Articles*, 2nd ed. Thousand Oaks, California: Corwin Press, p. 16. Reprinted by permission of Corwin Press and Sage Publications; **p. 24**, © The New Yorker Collection, 1960, Robert Kraus from cartoonbank.com. All rights reserved; **p. 28**, Copyright 2003 by Randy Glasbergen, www.glasbergen.com; **p. 37**, Copyright Grantland Enterprises, www.grantland.net; **pp. 39–40**, Adapted with permission from SEDL. Source: Hord, S. M., Rutherford, W. L., Huling, L., & Hall, G. E. (2006). *Taking Charge of Change* (Revised ed.), Austin, Texas: SEDL; **p. 40**, Copyright Grantland Enterprises, www.grantland.net; **p. 43**, www.CartoonStock.com; **p. 45**, Peanuts: © United Feature Syndicate, Inc.; **p. 51**, © The New Yorker Collection, 1973, Henry Martin from cartoonbank.com. All rights reserved; **pp. 51–52** (bullets), Courtesy of Eye on Education; **p. 56**, © Tribune Media Services, Inc. All Rights Reserved. Reprinted with permission; **p. 60**, www.CartoonStock.com; **p. 74**, CALVIN AND HOBBES ©1993 Watterson. Dist. By UNIVERSAL PRESS SYNDICATE. Reprinted with permission. All rights reserved; **p. 75**, CORNERED © 2006 Mike Baldwin. Reprinted with permission of UNIVERSAL PRESS SYNDICATE. All rights reserved; **p. 89**, www.CartoonStock.com; **p. 90**, CALVIN AND HOBBES © 1993 Watterson. Dist. By UNIVERSAL PRESS SYNDICATE. Reprinted with permission. All rights reserved; **pp. 93–95, 97–100** (Chapter 7 PowerPoints), from *Understanding by Design*, 2nd ed. (p. 151), by Jay McTighe and Grant Wiggins. Alexandria, Virginia: ASCD, 2004. Used with permission. The Association for Supervision and Curriculum Development is a worldwide community of educators advocating sound policies and sharing best practices to achieve the success of each learner. To learn more, visit ASCD at www.ascd.org; **p. 102**, Peanuts: © United Feature Syndicate, Inc.; **p. 116**, Adapted by permission of McREL from *Classroom Instruction that Works: Research-Based Strategies for Increasing Student Achievement*; **p. 117**, Copyright Grantland Enterprises, www.grantland.net; **pp. 119–120**, Reprinted with permission from *When Kids Can't Read* by Kylene Beers. Copyright © 2003 by Kylene Beers. Published by Heinemann, Portsmouth, NH. All rights reserved; **p. 133**, Peanuts: © United Feature Syndicate, Inc.; **p. 151**, Peanuts: © United Feature Syndicate, Inc.; **p. 155**, Copyright Grantland Enterprises, www.grantland.net; **p. 156**, Copyright Grantland Enterprises, www.grantland.net.